Experiencing Choral Music

ADVANCED

MIXED

Developed by

HAL•LEONARD® CORPORATION

Glencoe

New York, New York   Columbus, Ohio   Chicago, Illinois   Peoria, Illinois   Woodland Hills, California

The portions of the National Standards for Music Education included here are reprinted from *National Standards for Arts Education* with permission from MENC—The National Association for Music Education. All rights reserved. Copyright © 1994 by MENC. The complete National Standards and additional materials relating to the Standards are available from MENC, 1806 Robert Fulton Drive, Reston, VA 20191 (telephone 800-336-3768).

A portion of the sales of this material goes to support music education programs through programs of MENC—The National Association for Music Education.

 **Glencoe**

The *McGraw·Hill* Companies

Printed in the United States of America.

Send all inquiries to:
Glencoe/McGraw-Hill
21600 Oxnard Street, Suite 500
Woodland Hills, CA 91367

ISBN 0-07-861129-6 (Student Edition)
ISBN 0-07-861130-x (Teacher Wraparound Edition)

7 8 9 045 09 08 07

Credits

LEAD AUTHORS

Emily Crocker
Vice President of Choral Publications
Hal Leonard Corporation, Milwaukee, Wisconsin
Founder and Artistic Director, Milwaukee Children's Choir

Michael Jothen
Professor of Music, Program Director of Graduate Music Education
Chairperson of Music Education
Towson University, Towson, Maryland

Jan Juneau
Choral Director
Klein Collins High School
Spring, Texas

Henry H. Leck
Associate Professor and Director of Choral Activities
Butler University, Indianapolis, Indiana
Founder and Artistic Director, Indianapolis Children's Choir

Michael O'Hern
Choral Director
Lake Highlands High School
Richardson, Texas

Audrey Snyder
Composer
Eugene, Oregon

Mollie Tower
Coordinator of Choral and General Music, K-12, Retired
Austin, Texas

AUTHORS

Anne Denbow
Voice Instructor, Professional Singer/Actress
Director of Music, Holy Cross Episcopal Church
Simpsonville, South Carolina

Rollo A. Dilworth
Director of Choral Activities and Music
  Education
North Park University, Chicago, Illinois

Deidre Douglas
Choral Director
Aragon Middle School, Houston, Texas

Ruth E. Dwyer
Associate Director and Director of Education
Indianapolis Children's Choir
Indianapolis, Indiana

Norma Freeman
Choral Director
Saline High School, Saline, Michigan

Cynthia I. Gonzales
Music Theorist
Greenville, South Carolina

Michael Mendoza
Professor of Choral Activities
New Jersey State University
Trenton, New Jersey

Thomas Parente
Associate Professor
Westminster Choir College of Rider University
Princeton, New Jersey

Barry Talley
Director of Fine Arts and Choral Director
Deer Park ISD, Deer Park, Texas

CONTRIBUTING AUTHORS

Debbie Daniel
Choral Director, Webb Middle School
Garland, Texas

Roger Emerson
Composer/Arranger
Mount Shasta, California

Kari Gilbertson
Choral Director, Forest Meadow Junior High
Richardson, Texas

Tim McDonald
Creative Director, Music Theatre International
New York, New York

Christopher W. Peterson
Assistant Professor of Music Education (Choral)
University of Wisconsin-Milwaukee
Milwaukee, Wisconsin

Kirby Shaw
Composer/Arranger
Ashland, Oregon

Stephen Zegree
Professor of Music
Western Michigan State University
Kalamazoo, Michigan

EDITORIAL

Linda Rann
Senior Editor
Hal Leonard Corporation
Milwaukee, Wisconsin

Stacey Nordmeyer
Choral Editor
Hal Leonard Corporation
Milwaukee, Wisconsin

Table of Contents

Introductory Materials .... i–viii

Lessons

1 **Jubilate Deo • SATB** 2
   Joel Martinson

2 **Flower Of Beauty • SATB** 12
   John Clements

3 **Benedicamus Domino • SATB** 18
   Peter Warlock

   Spotlight On Physiology Of The Voice 25

4 **No Rocks A-Cryin' • SATB** 26
   Rollo A. Dilworth

5 **What Sweeter Music • SATB divisi** 34
   John Rutter

   Spotlight On Gospel Music 43

6 **S'vivon • SATB** 44
   Traditional Chanukah Song, arranged by Bob Chilcott

7 **Lux Aurumque • SATB divisi** 50
   Eric Whitacre

   Spotlight On Physiology Of Singing 57

8 **Noèl Ayisyen • SATB** 58
   Emile Desamours

9 **Il est bel et bon • SATB** 72
   Pierre Passereau, edited by J. S. Jackman

10 **Domine Fili Unigenite • SATB** 82
    Antonio Vivaldi, edited by Mason Martens

11 **Sancta Maria, mater Dei, K. 273 • SATB** 94
    Wolfgang Amadeus Mozart, edited by Denis McCaldin

Spotlight On Arranging 105

12   Zigeunerleben • SATB 106
     Robert Schuman

Spotlight On Concert Etiquette 122

Music & History

Renaissance Period 124

Baroque Period 128

Classical Period 132

Romantic Period 136

Contemporary Period 140

Spotlight On Musical Theater 144

Choral Library

America, The Beautiful • SATB divisi 146
   Samuel A. Ward, arranged by John Leavitt

Ave Maria • SATB divisi 158
   Javier Busto

Dörven Dalai • SATB 164
   Inner Mongolian Folk Song, arranged by Yongrub

I'm Gonna Sing 'Til The Spirit Moves
In My Heart • SATB divisi 172
   Moses Hogan

Spotlight On Careers In Music 185

If Music Be The Food Of Love • SATB 186
   David C. Dickau

The Last Words Of David • SATB 198
Randall Thompson

Pingos D'água • SATB 208
Henrique de Curitiba, edited by Eduardo Lakschevitz
and Henry Leck

Spotlight On Improvisation 215

A Rose Touched By The Sun's Warm Rays • SATB 216
Jean Berger

Set Me As A Seal • SATB divisi 220
René Clausen

Skylark • SATB 226
Hoagy Carmichael, arranged by Mac Huff

Spotlight On Vocal Jazz 235

Somewhere from *West Side Story* • SATB divisi 236
Leonard Bernstein, arranged by Robert Edgerton

Spotlight On Vocal Health 245

Sorida • SATB divisi 246
Rosephanye Powell

Glossary 263

Classified Index 279

Index of Songs and Spotlights 281

TO THE STUDENT

Welcome to choir!

By singing in the choir, you have chosen to be a part of an exciting and rewarding adventure. The benefits of being in choir are many. Basically, singing is fun. It provides an expressive way of sharing your feelings and emotions. Through choir, you will have friends that share a common interest with you. You will experience the joy of making beautiful music together. Choir provides the opportunity to develop your interpersonal skills. It takes teamwork and cooperation to sing together, and you must learn how to work with others. As you critique your individual and group performances, you can improve your ability to analyze and communicate your thoughts clearly.

Even if you do not pursue a music career, music can be an important part of your life. There are many avocational opportunities in music. **Avocational** means *not related to a job or career*. Singing as a hobby can provide you with personal enjoyment, enrich your life, and teach you life skills. Singing is something you can do for the rest of your life.

In this course, you will be presented with the basic skills of vocal production and music literacy. You will be exposed to songs from different cultures, songs in many different styles and languages, and songs from various historical periods. You will discover connections between music and the other arts. Guidelines for becoming a better singer and choir member include:

- Come to class prepared to learn.
- Respect the efforts of others.
- Work daily to improve your sight-singing skills.
- Sing expressively at all times.
- Have fun singing.

This book was written to provide you with a meaningful choral experience. Take advantage of the knowledge and opportunities offered here. Your exciting adventure of experiencing choral music is about to begin!

Lessons

Lessons for the Beginning of the Year

1   Jubilate Deo **2**

2   Flower Of Beauty **12**

3   Benedicamus Domino **18**

4   No Rocks A-Cryin' **26**

Lessons for Mid-Winter

5   What Sweeter Music **34**

6   S'vivon **44**

7   Lux Aurumque **50**

8   Noèl Ayisyen **58**

Lessons for Concert/Festival

9   Il est bel et bon **72**

10   Domine Fili Unigenite **82**

11   Sancta Maria, mater Dei, K. 273 . . . . . . **94**

12   Zigeunerleben **106**

Jubilate Deo

Composer: Joel Martinson
Text: Psalm 100
Voicing: SATB

VOCABULARY

meter

tonality

Contemporary
  period

fixed *do*

chromatic scale

Focus

- Perform music representing the Contemporary period.
- Identify and produce contrasting vocal tone colors.
- Read music using the fixed *do* system.

Getting Started

Think about the following questions:

1. What would Mona Lisa look like without her frame?

2. Where would Don Quixote be without Sancho Panza?

3. Would Godiva chocolate taste as good if it came in a plastic bag?

Sometimes greatness is surrounded by a support system that doesn't always get the credit it deserves. In "Jubilate Deo," you will see that the voice parts are strong, engaging and impressive statements. Closer inspection reveals an exciting keyboard/ organ accompaniment, which skillfully ties the vocal lines together and makes the accompaniment an equal partner. Singers know that behind every great performance is a fine accompanist.

SPOTLIGHT

To learn more about physiology of the voice, see page 25.

◆ History and Culture

After observing the accompaniment of "Jubilate Deo," it is not surprising to discover that Dallas, Texas, composer Joel Martinson is also an accomplished organist. Martinson has used the first line of "Psalm 100" for his title. *Jubilate Deo* means "Sing to the Lord." This composition overflows with celebration and joy. Excitement and vitality are created by several changes in **meter** (*the pattern into which a steady succession of rhythmic beats is organized*) and **tonality** (*the organized relationships of pitches with reference to a definite key center*). Tap a constant eighth note pulse as you work through the meter changes. Sometimes the tonality changes with each phrase. This makes "Jubilate Deo" a good example of music from the **Contemporary period** (*1900–present*).

Links to Learning

◆ ## Vocal

Because of the frequent tonality changes in "Jubilate Deo," learning to read the notation with the **fixed** *do* system (do *is always "C" regardless of the key signature*) may be helpful. Sing the **chromatic scale** (*a scale composed entirely of half steps*) shown below on solfège syllables. Keep the half step intervals very small to avoid singing sharp while ascending and singing flat while descending.

◆ ## Artistic Expression

The keyboard/organ accompaniment and chromatic alterations give "Jubilate Deo" a great deal of musical color. What visual colors would you associate with the various musical colors? Write out the text of "Jubilate Deo" using different fonts and colors to represent the musical setting of the words. Include dynamic and expressive markings in the color score. Follow your color score as you sing, and change your vocal tone color to match the score.

Evaluation

Demonstrate how well you have learned the skills and concepts featured in the lesson "Jubilate Deo" by completing the following:

- In an SATB quartet, sing measures 41–51 using the fixed *do* system. Evaluate your ability to sing with accurate intonation.

- In double SATB quartets, perform "Jubilate Deo" while following one singer's color score from Artistic Expression. Choose stylistic preferences for interpretation of the color score. Evaluate the effectiveness of your performance.

Composed for Temple Emanu-El's Interfaith Service, 1991, and dedicated to the participating choirs, music directors, rabbis and clergy

Jubilate Deo

For SATB and Keyboard/Organ

Psalm 100
Book of Common Prayer

JOEL MARTINSON

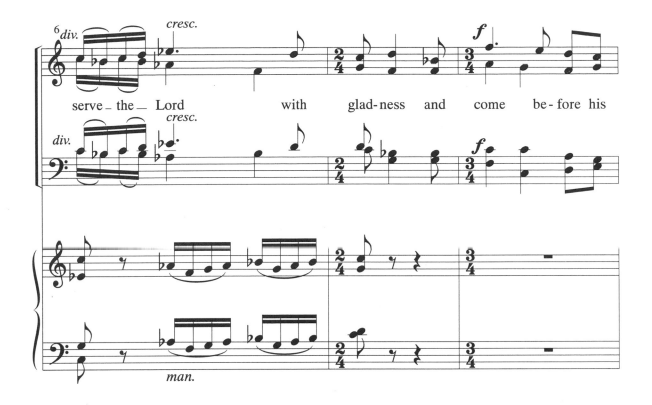

serve — the — Lord   with   glad-ness   and   come   be-fore his

man.

pres - ence with a song.

he him-self has made ——— us, ——————— and we are

his; we are his peo-ple and the

sheep — of his pas-ture.

pp   cresc.   rall.   *mf*

30   *Tempo I*   ♩ = 88

mf unis.

En - ter his gates   with   thanks -

mf unis.

(reg. as the beginning)

I   *f*

man.   ped.

Name.   For the Lord is

good; _____   rall.   his mer - cy   is

Flower Of Beauty

Composer: John Clements
Text: Sydney Bell
Voicing: SATB

VOCABULARY
strophic
suspension

Focus

- Identify and perform suspensions.
- Use musical expression to interpret poetry.

Getting Started

Are you familiar with these famous poems about flowers?

It is at the edge of a petal that love waits.
   William Carlos Williams, American poet (1883–1963)

When love came first to Earth, the Spring spread rose-beds to receive him.
   Thomas Campbell, Scottish poet (1777–1844)

My love is like a red, red rose that's newly sprung in June.
   Robert Burns, Scottish poet (1759–1796)

The fragrant, delicate beauty of nature's garden—can there be a more romantic gift than a bouquet of flowers? It might be a poet's words comparing one's beloved to a beautiful flower, or even greater, the setting of the poet's words to glorious music.

SPOTLIGHT

To learn more about concert etiquette, see page 122.

◆ History and Culture

Although composer John Clements has chosen a **strophic** setting *(a song in which all verses are sung to the same music)* for this poem, he gives careful attention to important words in the text. Find the word *shining* in measure 7. The placement of *shining* on the first beat and on high pitches gives it special emphasis. In addition, the effective use of **suspensions** *(the holding over of one or more musical tones in a chord into the following chord, producing a momentary discord)* produces a warm and intimate sound.

The first flower that blossomed on this earth was an invitation to an unborn song.

   Rabindanath Tagore, Indian writer (1861–1941)

Links to Learning

◆ **Theory**

Suspensions create the effect of tension and release in music. Locate the following suspensions in the music. Which voice part sings the suspended note? Practice each suspension using solfège syllables. Emphasize the dissonant note so it is the most prominent note of the chord. Then, sing the resolution note lighter to achieve a sensitive and expressive phrase ending.

◆ **Artistic Expression**

Write or type the words to "Flower Of Beauty" in verse form on a piece of paper. Recite the poem several times until you are satisfied with a reading that expresses your interpretation of the words. Underline the words you emphasized. Find the underlined words in the song and decide how you can musically emphasize each word.

Evaluation

Demonstrate how well you have learned the skills and concepts featured in the lesson "Flower Of Beauty" by completing the following:

- Sing your voice part in measures 1–17 a cappella, demonstrating musical emphasis of the text. Ask a classmate to listen and identify which words you chose to emphasize. Switch roles.

- Write or find a line of poetry about flowers. Compose a melody for the words. Add a harmonic line that includes one suspension. Sing your composition with a classmate. Check your work for rhythmic and harmonic accuracy. How well did you do?

Flower Of Beauty

For SATB, a cappella

Words by
SYDNEY BELL

Music by
JOHN CLEMENTS

know she walks in the eve-ning down by the ri-ver-side, And the grass-es lean to

know she walks in the eve-ning down __ by __ the ri-ver-side, __ And the grass-es lean to

know she walks in the eve-ning down by __ the ri-ver-side, And the grass-es lean to

know she walks in the eve-ning down by the ri-ver-side, And the grass-es lean to

kiss her robes who soon __ will be my bride: More dear to me her lit-tle head than

kiss her robes __ who soon will be my bride: More __ dear to me her lit-tle head than __

kiss her robes who soon will be my bride: __ More __ dear to me her lit-tle head __ than

kiss her robes who soon will be my bride: More dear to me her lit-tle head than

Benedicamus Domino

Composer: Peter Warlock (1894–1930)
Text: Poem from *Sloane Manuscript 2593*
Voicing: SATB

VOCABULARY

diphthong

liturgical Latin

International
   Phonetic
   Alphabet

Focus

• Perform music expressively with the use of syllabic stress.

• Read and sing a Latin text using IPA.

Getting Started

e pluribus unum … carpe diem … semper fideles … et cetera … vice versa

Although no longer a common spoken language, Latin is certainly present in modern culture. Can you translate the common Latin expressions shown above? Pure vowels and the absence of **diphthongs** (*a combination of two vowel sounds consisting of a primary vowel sound and a secondary vowel sound*) make Latin a favorite language for singers. If you study Latin in school, however, the pronunciation in class may be different from the pronunciation at choir rehearsals. Choral music uses church Latin, or **liturgical Latin** (*based on early Roman vernacular or common usage*), while Latin students learn classical Latin (the language of Roman scholars, writers and poets). The text of "Benedicamus Domino" ("Let Us Give Praise Unto The Lord") is written in liturgical Latin.

◆ History and Culture

The fact that English composer Peter Warlock (1894–1930) was also a Medieval and Renaissance scholar may be the reason he chose this fifteenth-century poem for such a rhythmic and joyful setting. Warlock wrote in 1926,

> "…music is neither old nor modern; it is either good or bad music, and the date at which it was written has no significance whatever… All good music, whatever its date, is ageless—as alive and significant today as it was when it was written…"

SKILL BUILDERS

To learn more about dotted rhythms, see Advanced Sight-Singing, *see pages 53–54.*

Links to Learning

◆ Vocal

The **International Phonetic Alphabet, or IPA,** *is a system that gives a symbol for every sound.* First developed in 1886, it is found in dictionaries and pronunciation guides. Here are the six Latin vowels with their IPA pronunciations.

a [ɑ] (f<u>a</u>ther)   e [ɛ] (f<u>e</u>d)   i [i] (f<u>ee</u>t)   o [ɔ] (f<u>ou</u>ght)   u [u] (f<u>oo</u>d)   y [i] (f<u>ee</u>t)

Can you sing each vowel without any trace of a diphthong?

◆ Artistic Expression

Find the refrain *Gloria! Laudes!* in the music. Warlock sets these two words with careful attention to syllabic stress. He places the first syllable of each word on beat one and gives it the highest pitch of the measure. Recite the Latin text in measures 1–11 with the correct syllabic stress. Stress the underlined syllables.

<u>pro</u>-ce-<u>den</u>-ti <u>pu</u>-e-ro <u>e</u>-ya <u>no</u>-bis <u>ann</u>-us est!

<u>vir</u>-gin-is ex <u>u</u>-te-ro <u>glo</u>-ri a! <u>lau</u>-des!

<u>de</u>-us <u>ho</u>-mo <u>fac</u>-tus est et <u>im</u>-<u>mor</u>-<u>ta</u>-lis.

Evaluation

Demonstrate how well you have learned the skills and concepts featured in the lesson "Benedicamus Domino" by completing the following:

- Write out the text for "Benedicamus Domino" measures 1–22 using IPA for all the vowels. Ask a classmate to check your pronunciation as you sing your voice part. Evaluate how well you are able to identify IPA pronunciations.

- Sing into a microphone and record yourself singing "Benedicamus Domino." Listen to your recording and assess how well you were able to sing the Latin text with correct syllabic stress.

Benedicamus Domino

For SATB, a cappella

Liturgical Latin

Music by
PETER WARLOCK

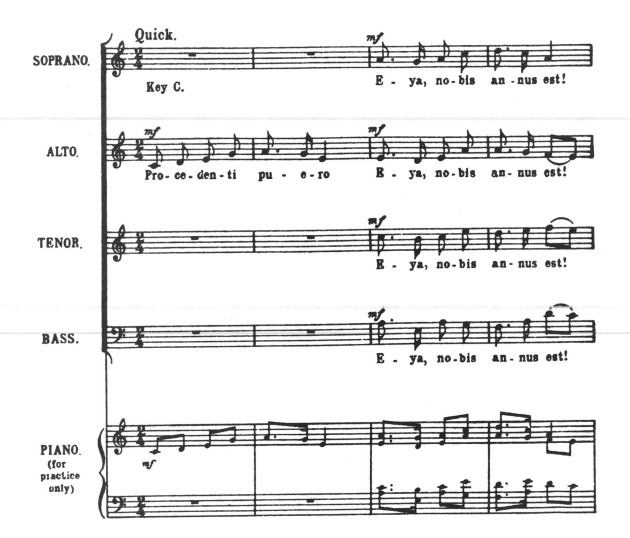

Physiology Of The Voice

Physiology is a branch of biology that deals with living organisms and their parts. It is interesting to see how the parts of the human body work together to produce vocal sound. Vocal production requires the following elements:

The Actuators

The actuators are parts of the body involved in the breathing process. The parts of the airway include (1) head airways (the nose and mouth), (2) pharynx (throat tube), (3) larynx (voice box), (4) trachea (windpipe), (5) bronchi (two branches of trachea that lead into the lungs), and (6) lungs. The muscles used in breathing include (1) the abdominals (belly muscles), (2) intercostals (muscles attached to the ribs), and (3) diaphragm (a horizontal, dome-shaped muscle separating the chest and abdominal cavities).

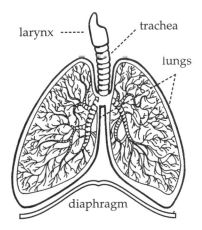

The Vibrators

The vocal folds (or "vocal cords") are housed in the larynx (the voice box) at the top of the trachea and vibrate when air from the lungs passes between them.

The Resonators

The sound waves produced by the vocal folds are enhanced and amplified by the resonators, or natural cavities located in the pharynx, larynx, mouth, nasal passages and sinus passages.

The Articulators

The articulators are the parts of the body used in speech, namely the lips, teeth, tongue, jaw and soft palate. To find the soft palate, place the tip of your tongue on the roof of your mouth and slide it toward your throat just past the bony ridge of your hard palate.

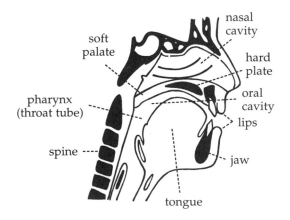

No Rocks A-Cryin'

Composer: Rollo A. Dilworth
Text: Based on Psalm 47, with additional words by Rollo A. Dilworth
Voicing: SATB

VOCABULARY

gospel music

swell

Focus

- Describe characteristics of gospel music.

- Sing expressively using techniques specific to the gospel style.

- Perform music representing the American heritage.

SPOTLIGHT

To learn more about gospel music, see page 43.

Getting Started

In nature, animals are classified by certain characteristics. For example, you might rationalize that you are looking at a bird because of the physical characteristics, including a beak, feathers and wings. Although it is a bird, there are many types of birds— some have a uniform color, while others have an array of brilliant colors. In music, we classify songs based on their characteristics and style. "No Rocks A-Cryin'" is classified as **gospel music,** *religious music that originated in the African American churches of the South and which is characterized by improvisation, syncopation and repetition.* Some gospel songs consist of basic harmonies and rhythms, while others incorporate more elaborate harmonies and complex rhythmic patterns. In "No Rocks A-Cryin'," you will explore a mixture of both simple and complex harmonies, along with unison and imitative passages.

◆ History and Culture

Gospel music has been in existence since the 1930s. A blues musician and songwriter named Thomas A. Dorsey (1899–1993) is known as the "father of gospel music." His songs consisted of simple harmonic progressions and regular four-bar phrases that helped to establish the traditional gospel sound. In the late 1960s, Walter Hawkins pioneered a new gospel sound that incorporated more complex harmonies reminiscent of modern rock and jazz music. His song "Oh Happy Day" became known as the groundbreaking chart for the contemporary gospel movement. Today, both traditional and contemporary gospel styles are very popular.

Links to Learning

◆ Theory

Read and perform the following rhythmic example to practice syncopated patterns. Stress the accented notes. When you have mastered the pattern, chant the text.

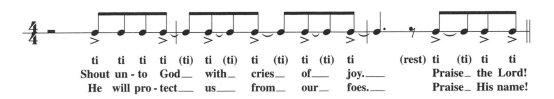

ti	ti	ti	ti	(ti)	ti	(ti)	ti	(ti)	ti	(ti)	ti	(rest)	ti	(ti)	ti	ti

Shout un-to God__ with__ cries__ of__ joy.__ Praise_ the Lord!

He will pro-tect__ us__ from__ our__ foes.__ Praise_ His name!

◆ Artistic Expression

After you are secure in the pitch and rhythms of the first verse (measures 6–24), add the following performance techniques that are common in the African American gospel style:

- Chant with a percussive style (non-legato, but not staccato). This technique will enhance the rhythmic vitality of the piece.

- Add a **swell** *(a somewhat breathy, sudden crescendo)* to words or syllables that deserve dramatic emphasis ("hands," "joy" and "worthy").

- Textual repetitions should either increase or decrease slightly in dynamic level. As you repeat the phrase "I don't want the rocks" (measures 20 and 22), increase the dynamic level slightly.

Evaluation

Demonstrate how well you have learned the skills and concepts featured in the lesson "No Rocks A-Cryin'" by completing the following:

- Listen to a recording of "No Rocks A-Cryin" and describe the characteristics of gospel music found in this piece. Compare your list with a classmate's. Why should this song be classified as gospel style?

- Sing with an expressive style that employs the techniques that are characteristic of the African American gospel tradition.

- In a small ensemble, perform this song. Evaluate your performance based on the expressive techniques described in the Artistic Expression section above. How well were you able to sing in an authentic gospel style?

Dedicated to the Providence – St. Mel School Choirs of Chicago, Illinois
David Baar, Conductor

No Rocks A-Cryin'

For SATB and Piano

Based on Psalm 47

Words and Music by
ROLLO A. DILWORTH

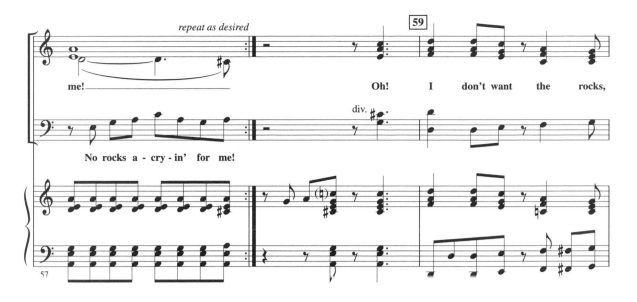

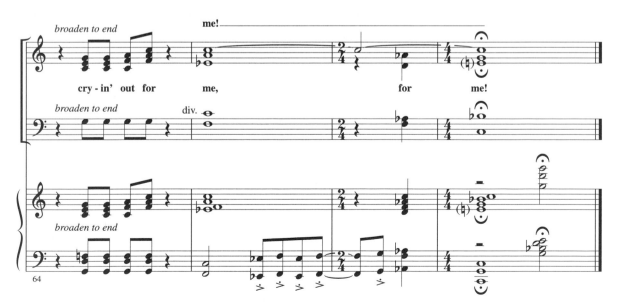

What Sweeter Music

Composer: John Rutter
Text: Robert Herrick
Voicing: SATB divisi

VOCABULARY

arranger

diatonic interval

Focus

- Perform music representing the Contemporary period.
- Analyze and describe characteristics of musical composition.
- Analyze and sing melodic intervals.

Getting Started

Can you sing music in your head? Before singing "What Sweeter Music," take a good look at the melody, harmony and rhythm. As you read the music silently, jot down four adjectives you think will best describe the sound and style. Now look for these specific lyrics:

1. *"awake the voice!"*
2. *"dark and dull night, fly hence away"*
3. *"thus on the sudden?"*
4. *"the darling of the world is come"*

Without singing out loud again, write down a few words to describe how composer John Rutter has used the music to strengthen the meaning of these lyrics. When you analyze how a piece of choral music is written, you are thinking like a composer or an **arranger** *(a composer who takes an original or existing melody and adds extra features or changes the melody in some way).*

 **SPOTLIGHT**

To learn more about careers in music, see page 185.

◆ History and Culture

The poem "What Sweeter Music" was written by English clergyman and poet Robert Herrick (1591–1674). Seventeenth-century England heard the poem sung at Christmastime to a German melody. The resulting song has been known as "Herrick's Carol" ever since. Englishman John Rutter (b. 1945) is one of several contemporary composers who have given the poem a new setting. Mr. Rutter is a busy conductor, record producer, choral music specialist and music anthologist, but is best known as a composer and arranger of Christmas carols. Keep analyzing the elements of this beautiful and deeply moving carol, and you may be inspired to write a new setting for "Joy To The World" or "The Holly And The Ivy"!

Links to Learning

◆ **Theory**

The melody for "What Sweeter Music" is very unique; it contains every **diatonic interval** *(an interval that is based on a diatonic scale and uses no altered pitches or accidentals)* in the scale. There is at least one unison, second, third, fourth, fifth, sixth, seventh and octave. Copy the melody shown below on staff paper. Write in the solfège syllables and identify and label all indicated melodic intervals. Sing these intervals accurately and in tune.

◆ **Artistic Expression**

Referring to your list of adjectives and descriptions from Getting Started, make a list of vocal techniques you feel will add expressiveness to "What Sweeter Music." These might include "observing the dynamic markings" or "singing with syllabic stress." Make vocal technique flash cards to be used while learning this song by writing each technique on a large piece of paper.

Evaluation

Demonstrate how well you have learned the skills and concepts featured in the lesson "What Sweeter Music" by completing the following:

- In a comfortable octave, sing measures 4–12 on solfège syllables, demonstrating ability to sing all diatonic intervals smoothly and accurately.

- Compose a new melody for the text *"What sweeter music …awake the string!"* in G♭ major and **¾** meter. Include at least three melodic intervals from measures 4–12. Evaluate how well you understand melodic intervals.

For Stephen Cleobury and
the choir of King's College, Cambridge

What Sweeter Music

For SATB divisi and Organ

Words by
ROBERT HERRICK (1591–1674)

JOHN RUTTER

mea-dow new-ly shorn Thus on the sud - den? Come and see The cause, why

'Tis he is born, whose quick-'ning birth Gives life and

things thus fra-grant be: 'Tis he is born, whose quick-'ning birth Gives life and

lu - stre, pub-lic mirth,_ To hea-ven and the un-der-earth. We see him

lu - stre, pub-lic mirth, To hea-ven and the un-der-earth.

(Man.)

sing The birth of this our heav'n-ly King, the birth of

sing The birth of this our heav'n-ly King. (Hum)

sing The birth of this our heav'n-ly King. (Hum)

sing The birth of this our heav'n-ly King. (Hum)

this our hea – ven-ly King.

(Ped.)

SPOTLIGHT

Gospel Music

Gospel music is *religious music that originated in the African American churches of the South.* Characteristics of gospel music include improvisation, syncopation and repetition. Following the Civil War, African American churches began to emerge. The spirituals sung by the early slaves served as their main source of sacred music. By the early 1900s, some sectors of the church moved to more spirited songs accompanied by tambourines, drums and piano. These were the earliest versions of gospel music.

African American gospel music gained national recognition during the 1940s and the 1950s with the recordings and live concerts of the singing great Mahalia Jackson. Also influential was Thomas Andrew Dorsey (1899–1993). He published over 400 gospel songs and is known as the father of gospel music. His gospel music used lively rhythms and syncopated piano accompaniments. "Precious Lord, Take My Hand" is probably his most famous song.

When asked about the correct way to sing gospel music, contemporary composer Rollo Dilworth shared these thoughts. He said that singers often debate about the appropriate use of chest voice and head voice registers when performing gospel style. While some believe that excessive use of the chest voice might cause vocal damage, others believe that singing in the African American idiom is not "authentic" if performed in head voice. Dilworth suggests that successful singing in most any genre requires a balanced, healthy singing tone in both head and chest registers.

Vocal techniques used in gospel singing include (1) percussive singing (a style that lies between legato and staccato styles); (2) swell (an exaggerated crescendo that adds weight and breadth to an accented syllable); and (3) pitch bending (or the scooping up to a pitch, often coupled with a swell or "falling off" of a pitch). The rhythm is felt in an accurate yet relaxed style. Basic movements may include stepping, clapping and rocking. Improvisation of melody is frequently heard in gospel music.

Listen to a recording of other gospel music and identify characteristics of gospel-style singing.

S'vivon

Composer: Traditional Chanukah Song, arranged by Bob Chilcott
Text: Traditional
Voicing: SATB

VOCABULARY

intonation

syncopation

Focus

- Singing with a tone that is appropriate for the style of the piece.
- Distinguishing between melodic and accompaniment material.
- Relating music to history and culture.

SPOTLIGHT

To learn more about arranging, see page 105.

Getting Started

To learn more about a culture, it is important to look at its music. The music reflects the customs, beliefs and traditions of that culture. The Chanukah song "S'vivon" reveals to us some important information regarding the customs and practices of the Jewish tradition.

◆ History and Culture

"S'vivon" is a traditional song that is usually sung by children during Chanukah. Chanukah, known as the feast of dedication and festival of lights, celebrates the victory of Judas Maccabee over the Syrian Greek army of Antiochus in 165 B.C. After the battle, the Hebrew people returned to their temple to rededicate it and found enough oil to kindle the temple's perpetual light for only one day. Miraculously, the oil lasted eight days! In remembrance of this miracle, the Jewish people celebrate Chanukah by lighting a candle on each of the eight nights to represent the eight days of the burning flame.

S'vivon is the Hebrew word for "dreidel," a small top that children spin. On each side of the top is a letter: **N** (Nun); **G** (Gimel); **H** (Hey); and **S** (Shin). The four Hebrew letters stand for the phrase *Nes Gadol Hayah Sham*, which means "A great miracle happened there."

The following is an English translation of the Hebrew text:

S'vivon, sov sov sov	Dreidel, spin, spin, spin,
Chanukah hu hag tov	Chanukah, it is a good holiday,
Chag simcha hu la-am	A happy holiday for our people,
Nes gadol hayah sham	A great miracle happened there.

Links to Learning

◆ Vocal

Sing the following vocal exercise to gain familiarity with the harmonies that you will find in the piece. Use a soft, bright and clear singing tone so that the pitches will blend together smoothly. Work for precise **intonation,** or *in-tune singing.*

◆ Theory

Clap, chant or tap the following rhythmic pattern with **syncopation** *(placing an accent off the beat or on the weaker portion of the beat).* Notice that the syncopation occurs on the weak portion of the beat (beats 3, 1 and 2) following a rest.

◆ Artistic Expression

Sing the Soprano, Alto and Tenor parts in measures 1–9. Next, sing the Alto, Tenor and Bass parts in measures 10–15. Identify which parts sing the melody, and which parts sing an accompaniment. Compare answers with a classmate. How well did you do?

Evaluation

Demonstrate how well you have learned the skills and concepts featured in the lesson "S'vivon" by completing the following:

- Critique a recording of the choir's performance of "S'vivon." Evaluate how well the choir was able to sing with a light and soft tone.

- Identify the passages in the music that contain the melody versus those passages that contain vocal accompaniment. Compare your answers with those of another classmate. How well did you do?

- Discuss the significance of this piece in the Jewish culture.

S'vivon

For SATB and Piano

Arranged by
BOB CHILCOTT

Traditional Chanukah Song

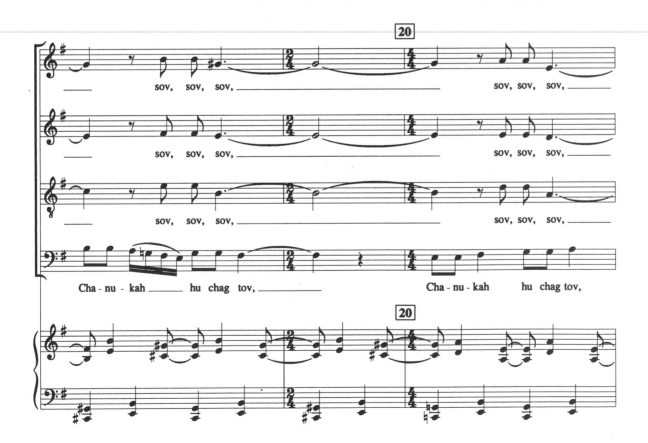

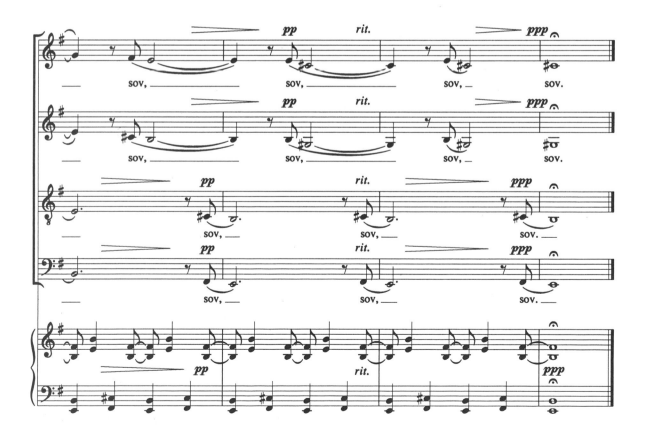

Lux Aurumque

Composer: Eric Whitacre
Text: Edward Esch
Voicing: SATB divisi

VOCABULARY

word painting

Contemporary period

dissonance

Focus

- Sing expressively music that features close harmonies and dissonance.
- Perform music representing the Contemporary period.
- Perform music written by American composers.

Getting Started

If you were living in Germany in the year 1875, and your choir was performing a song written by Johannes Brahms (1833–1897), Mr. Brahms might have been in attendance at your performance. Similarly, if you were one of the singers in the premiere of a W. A. Mozart (1756–1791) masterpiece in the year 1775, what an honor that would be! Today, singers have the opportunity to sing music of contemporary composers such as Eric Whitacre (b. 1970), one of the brightest young composers in America. "Lux Aurumque" was written in 2001.

MUSIC & HISTORY

To learn more about the Contemporary period, see page 140.

◆ History and Culture

Whitacre is a master of **word painting**—*a technique in which the music reflects the meaning of the words.* He took a simple poem by American poet Charles Anthony Silvestri and had it translated into Latin for the setting of this text. The English translation is as follows:

> *Light,*
>
> *warm and heavy as pure gold*
>
> *and the angels sing softly*
>
> *to the new-born baby.*

"Lux Aurumque" is an example of music written in the **Contemporary period** *(1900–present).* The composer has chosen to write the piece using very close harmony and **dissonance** *(a combination of pitches or tones that clash)* to describe *light.* The composer suggests that "a simple approach is essential to the success of the work, and if the tight harmonies are carefully tuned and balanced, they will shimmer and glow."

Links to Learning

◆ **Vocal**

Perform the following example as a daily warm-up. Sing on a neutral syllable. Listen for the tension as the notes move into dissonance and then the release at the cadence. Can you find similar harmonic patterns in "Lux Aurumque"?

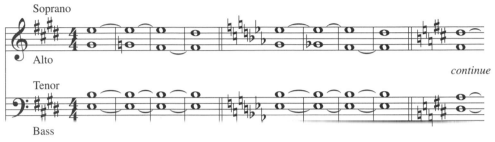

continue

◆ **Theory**

Perform the following example on solfège or neutral syllables to practice singing in close harmony. Keep the pitch centered as the other sections sing dissonance against your pitch.

Evaluation

Demonstrate how well you have learned the skills and concepts featured in the lesson "Lux Aurumque" by completing the following:

- Listen to a recording of your choir's performance of "Lux Aurumque." Listen carefully and evaluate how well your section was able to keep the pitch centered as other sections moved into dissonance with your part. Did the performance reflect the word *light* through expressive singing and phrasing?

- Find other examples of contemporary works in this textbook. Compare and contrast the works and decide what makes "Lux Aurumque" an exemplary work.

Commissioned by the Master Chorale of Tampa Bay
Lux Aurumque
For SATB divisi, a cappella

Words by EDWARD ESCH
Latin translation by
CHARLES ANTHONY SILVESTRI

ERIC WHITACRE

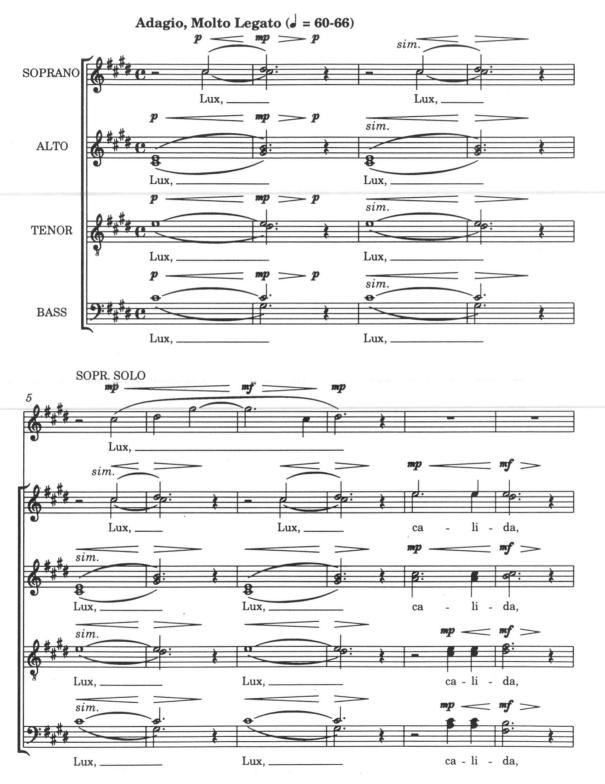

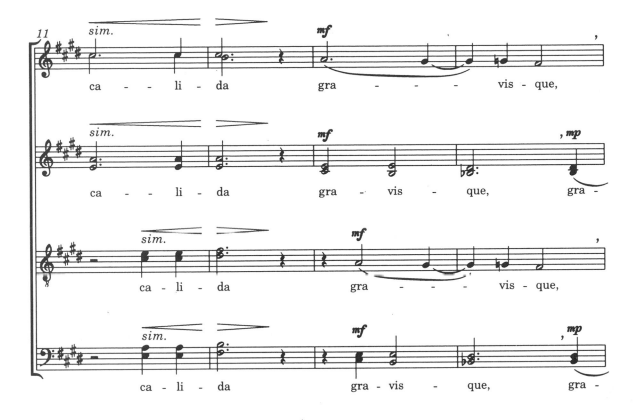

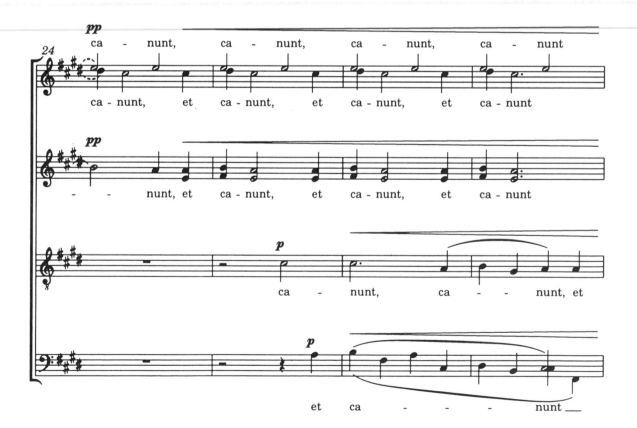

A Tempo

SPOTLIGHT

Physiology Of Singing

Physiology is a branch of biology that deals with living organisms and their parts. It is interesting to see how the parts of the human body affect our singing. Familiarize yourself with "Physiology of the Voice" on page 25 before studying this page.

Vocal Pitch, Range and Timbre

- Pitch is related to the length of the vocal folds. The longer and more stretched the folds are, the higher the pitch; the shorter and more relaxed, the lower the pitch.

- Range is related to the length and thickness of the vocal folds. Longer, thinner folds vibrate more easily at higher pitches; shorter, thicker folds vibrate more easily at lower pitches.

- Timbre or "tone color" of the voice is related to the size of the larynx, the relative thickness of the vocal folds, and resonance factors (see below). A large larynx with thicker vocal folds produces a deeper, richer sound; a small larynx with thinner vocal folds produces a lighter, simpler sound.

Resonance

- Resonance is related to the size, shape and texture of the surface of the resonators and how we utilize them.

- Some resonators are fixed in size, shape and texture; for example, the sinus and nasal cavities (except when you have a cold!).

- Others, such as the oral, pharyngeal and laryngeal cavities, change depending on how we utilize the articulators in shaping the vowels and defining the consonants.

Projection

- Projection is related to many factors. Some of these factors include (1) the amount of air pressure used at the onset of the tone and throughout the phrase, (2) the utilization of the resonators, (3) the amount of tension in the body, (4) the health of the vocal mechanism, (5) the physical and emotional energy level of the singer, and (6) the acoustics of the room.

Noèl Ayisyen

Composer: Emile Desamours
Text: Emile Desamours
Voicing: SATB

VOCABULARY

ostinato

vaccin

manniboula

syncopation

Focus

- Perform music representing the Haitian culture.
- Perform syncopated rhythms with accuracy and steadiness of tempo.
- Simulate the sounds of instruments using the voice.

Getting Started

Christmas is a holiday that is celebrated by many cultures around the world. Throughout time a number of Christmas carols have been translated into multiple languages so that people of all cultural backgrounds could enjoy them. For example, did you know that "Silent Night" came from Germany and that its original title was "Stille Nacht"? Composers have continued to write new songs that are appropriate for the holiday season. "Noèl Ayisyen" is an original carol that characterizes the culture and music of Haiti.

 **SPOTLIGHT**

To learn more about the physiology of singing, see page 57.

◆ History and Culture

The country of Haiti is a republic of the West Indies, located to the southeast of Cuba. Port-au-Prince is the capital of Haiti. French is the predominant language of the country, along with a dialect of the language called Creole.

"Noèl Ayisyen" uses many **ostinato** patterns, *a rhythmic or melodic passage that is repeated continuously.* The vocal parts imitate a number of instruments, including banjo, maracas, vaccin, manniboula, and drums. The **vaccin** is *an instrument consisting of one or two sections of bamboo, blown with the lips like a brass instrument mouthpiece.* The **manniboula** is *a rustic pizzicato bass instrument consisting of a wooden resonance box with a rose window on its front panel, where there are three fixed metallic blades that sound when manipulated by the fingers of the player sitting on it.*

Links to Learning

◆ Vocal

"Noèl Ayisyen" is written in the key of F minor and uses many intervals that outline triads of the F minor scale. **Syncopation** (*the placement of accents on a weak beat, or a weak portion of the beat, or on a note or notes that do not normally receive extra emphasis*) is found throughout. Perform the following example while maintaining a steady eighth-note pulse.

◆ Theory

Perform the following examples in this manner: (1) Clap pattern A, observing all of the accent markings. Repeat until mastered. (2) Clap pattern B, which includes only the accented notes from pattern A. (3) Clap pattern C, which is an alternate notation of pattern B. Find pattern C in the music.

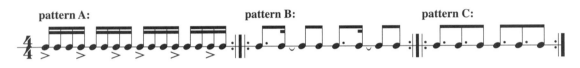

Compare patterns D and E. Are they the same or different? They are the same, but written in different notation. Perform pattern E first, then perform pattern D. Find examples similar to pattern D in the music.

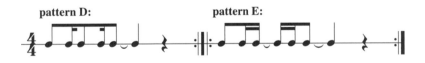

Evaluation

Demonstrate how well you have learned the skills and concepts featured in the lesson "Noèl Ayisyen" by completing the following:

- With one singer per part, perform the piece with all the correct rhythms, words, and percussive effects. Evaluate your ability to perform the syncopated rhythms with accuracy and steadiness of tempo.

- Perform measures 49–56 and pretend you are playing the vaccin, manniboula and other percussion instruments. While singing, show the movements you might make if you were playing the instruments. Sing the section on made-up sounds to imitate the instruments with your voice. Evaluate how well you were able to portray each instrument.

Noèl Ayisyen
(A Haitian Noël)

For SATB, a cappella

Words and Music by
EMILE DESAMOURS

+ *simulate vaccin playing*

* *Click tongue from roof to floor of mouth*

** *one person clap to emulate a "cracking" whip*

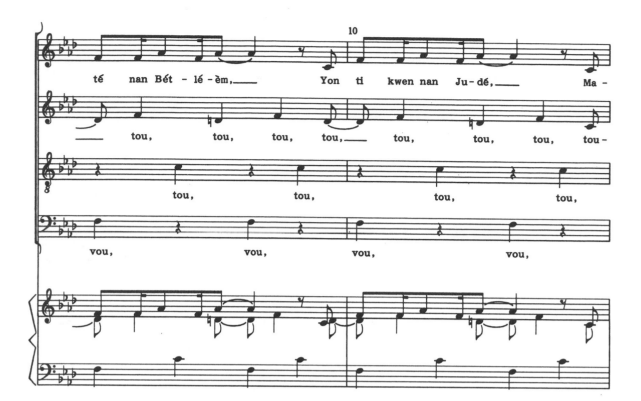

suiv yon gwo zé-twal,_ Ka-do yo nan men yo_ Pou yo vin' a-do-ré'l,_ É

tou, tou, tou, tou-lou, tou, tou, tou, tou-lou, tou, tou, tou, tou-

tou, tou, tou-lou,_ tou-lou-doup, tou, tou,

vou, vou, vou, vou, vou, vou, tou-

yo té byen sé-zi_____ Lè yo wè ti Jè-zi Kou-ché nan mi-

lou, tou, tou, tou, tou-lou, tou, tou. Kou-ché nan mi-

tou, tou, tou. Kou-ché nan mi-

lou, vou, vou, vou. Kou-ché nan mi-

* melody in the tenors in measures 25 to 28

*take care to balance this chord

* Click tongue from roof to floor of mouth

** clap as on page 2

* "tanm man nam" simulates banjo sound

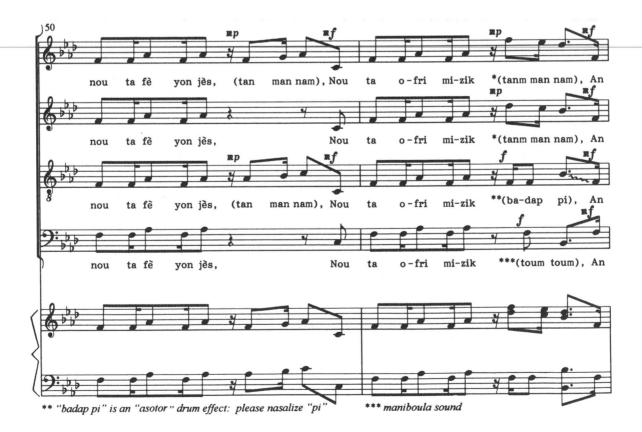

** "badap pi" is an "asotor" drum effect: please nasalize "pi"   *** maniboula sound

* (tchi-ki-tchi) is to be whispered, to emulate maracas sound

*claps progressively louder (mp-mf-f)

zi * (tan-man-nam). Jé - zi, Jé - zi, ti Jé - zi

zi * (tan-man-nam). Jé - zi, *(tan-man-nam, tam, tam-man-nam man nam, tan man

zi * (tan-man-nam). Jé - zi, *(tan-man-nam, tam, tam-man-nam man nam, tan man

zi * (tan-man-nam). Jé - zi, *(toum, toum, toum, toum, toum,

emulate instruments and, if possible, add gestures for the banjo

nou, A la ren-men, nou ren-men wou. Ou

nam, tan-man-nam, tam).— Vou, Nou ren-men wou. Hm

nam, tan-man-nam, tam).— Vou, Nou ren-men wou.

toum, toum).— Vou, Nou ren-men wou.

* *bring out contrasting rhythmic part in Soprano 2 and Alto*

Il est bel et bon

Composer: Pierre Passereau (c. 1509–1547), arranged by J. S. Jackman
Text: Traditional
Voicing: SATB

VOCABULARY

Renaissance period

chanson

polyphonic

homophony

Focus

- Define *chanson*. Perform a chanson using precise French diction.

- Describe *polyphony* and *homophony* and identify examples of each.

- Describe and perform music from the Renaissance period.

Getting Started

The Meredith Willson musical *The Music Man* (1957) tells the story of Harold Hill, a slick band-instrument salesman, who tries to swindle the decent folks of River City, Iowa. From the musical comes "Pick-a-little Talk-a-little," a song about gossip that goes back and forth between the ladies in town. Almost 400 years earlier, "Il est bel et bon," written during the **Renaissance period** *(c. 1430–1600)*, describes two women gossiping, or perhaps simply bragging, about their husbands "doing the housework and feeding the chickens." Convey this lighthearted and funny text to the audience as you perform this classic song about gossip.

MUSIC & HISTORY

To learn more about the Renaissance period, see page 124.

◆ History and Culture

"Il est bel et bon" ("He is good and handsome") was written by French composer Pierre Passereau (c. 1509–1547). It is an example of a **chanson,** *a vocal composition to French words that dates back to the late Middle Ages.* The French chansons were usually written in **polyphonic** style, *music consisting of two or more independent melodies, which combine to create simultaneous voice parts with different rhythms.* Differing from more traditional homophonic music, the polyphonic chansons involved close imitations, changes of pace and humorous texts. Passereau, known for his lively, impish and slightly obscene chansons, earned a place among the period's "merry musicians."

Links to Learning

◆ Vocal

Perform the following example with solfège syllables. Part I is written in D minor (beginning on *la*), while Part II is written in A minor (beginning on *la*). Sing with a gradual crescendo to the accented notes. Soprano/Tenor sing Part I, and Alto/Bass sing Part II. Switch parts and repeat.

Perform the following example to practice placing the accents in the correct place. Observe the accent markings and make a gradual crescendo to the accented notes. Find similar measures in the score.

◆ Theory

Homophony refers to *a texture in which there are two or more parts with similar or identical rhythms being sung at the same time.* Polyphony, on the other hand, is a texture in which two or more independent melodies that are different are sung together. Find an example of each of these textures in "Il est bel et bon."

Evaluation

Demonstrate how well you have learned the skills and concepts featured in the lesson "Il est bel et bon" by completing the following:

• With a classmate, practice speaking the French text. Evaluate how well you were able to speak with precise French diction.

• Compare "Il est bel et bon" with other Renaissance choral works. What characteristics are similar? Which are different? Identify if the music is written in a polyphonic or homophonic texture.

Il est bel et bon
(Look At My Impeccable Husband)

For SATB, a cappella

Edited with English Translation by
J. S. JACKMAN

PIERRE PASSEREAU

Domine Fili Unigenite

Composer: Antonio Vivaldi (1678–1741), edited by Mason Martens
Text: Liturgical Latin, English text by Mason Martens
Voicing: SATB

VOCABULARY

dotted rhythms

Baroque period

hemiola

Focus

- Read and perform dotted rhythms appropriate to the style of the music.

- Use standard terminology to define *hemiola*.

- Describe and perform music representing the Baroque period.

MUSIC & HISTORY

To learn more about the Baroque period, see page 128.

Getting Started

Antonio Vivaldi's "Domine Fili Unigenite" is a dynamic composition that features dotted rhythmic patterns throughout and, on occasion, double-dotted rhythms. **Dotted rhythms** are *pairs of notes, one of which is three times the length of the other.* Dotted rhythms are in the piano introduction and are also featured within the theme first sung by the Altos. In the Bass part, you will find a double-dotted quarter note. The first dot adds half the value of the quarter note; that is, an eighth note. The second dot adds half the value of the eighth note; that is, a sixteenth note. Were there a third dot, what value would it add?

◆ History and Culture

Antonio Vivaldi (1678–1741) is regarded as one of the most important Italian composers of the **Baroque period** *(1600–1750).* "Domine Fili Unigenite" is from his popular choral work *Gloria.* In addition to writing sacred music, Vivaldi composed over 500 concertos for solo instrument and orchestra. His most famous work in this genre is *The Four Seasons* for solo violin and orchestra. Although today we think of Vivaldi primarily as a composer, during his lifetime he was known as a violinist more than as a composer.

Music of the Baroque period had a dramatic flair and a strong sense of movement. The quiet a cappella style of the Renaissance gave way to large-scale productions and overall grandeur. Listen for these characteristics as you practice and perform "Domine Fili Unigenite."

Links to Learning

◆ **Vocal**

Sing the following excerpt to practice performing non-dotted rhythms and dotted rhythms. Be certain that the dotted eighth note is equal to the length of three sixteenth notes.

◆ **Theory**

A **hemiola** is *the ratio 2:3*. For example, hemiola occurs in ¾ meter when the strong beat shifts from occurring every three beats to occurring every two beats. Read and perform the following example by chanting the beat numbers as indicated and placing an accent on the number "1."

Evaluation

Demonstrate how well you have learned the skills and concepts featured in the lesson "Domine Fili Unigenite" by completing the following activities:

- Sing the main theme to demonstrate your ability to perform dotted rhythms accurately (Sopranos measures 18–26; Altos measures 9–17; Tenors measures 53–61; Basses measures 62–70). Evaluate how well you did.

- With a quartet, sing measures 79–84 to demonstrate your ability to perform a hemiola. Did the accent shift from every three beats to every two beats? Were you able to maintain a steady beat while shifting the placement of the accent?

Domine Fili Unigenite

For SATB and Piano

Liturgical Latin
Edited with English text by MASON MARTENS

ANTONIO VIVALDI
(1678–1741)

Soprano

Alto

Do - mi - ne__ Fi - li U - ni - ge - ni - te,__ Je -
On - ly - be - got - ten Lord and Son of__ God,__ Je -

Tenor

Bass

Do - mi - ne Fi - li U - ni - ge - ni - te,
On - ly - be - got - ten Lord and Son of God,

Sancta Maria, mater Dei

Composer: Wolfgang Amadeus Mozart (1756–1791), edited by Denis McCaldin
Text: Latin Antiphon
Voicing: SATB

VOCABULARY

Classical period

homophony

theme

tonic chord

dominant chord

Focus

- Through musical notation and performance, identify the main musical theme in a work.

- Identify tonic and dominant chords.

- Perform music representing the Classical period.

Getting Started

What do *balance, symmetry* and *unity* mean? Make a list of things in nature and in the world that exhibit these characteristics. Some suggestions to get you started might include butterflies, leaves of a tree, the Golden Gate Bridge and certain buildings. Discuss the physical aspects of these objects that classify them as having symmetry, balance and unity. These are also important elements of art, dance and music. "Sancta Maria, mater Dei" was composed during the **Classical period** *(1750–1820)* of Western musical history. Characteristics of the Classical period found in this piece include **homophony** *(a type of music in which there are two or more parts with similar or identical rhythms being sung at the same time)*, balance, and symmetry of form, as well as short four- and eight-bar phrases.

MUSIC&HISTORY

To learn more about the Classical period, see page 132.

◆ History and Culture

Wolfgang Amadeus Mozart (1756–1791) was born in Salzburg, Austria. By the age of five, he was a composer and keyboard virtuoso! He performed for many audiences, including royalty, when he toured Europe as a child. Mozart had an incredible musical gift that allowed him to compose music in his head before writing it down without a single mistake. Mozart composed more than 600 works before his death at the age of 35. "Sancta Maria, mater Dei" was written on 1777 for the feast of the Holy Name of Mary.

Links to Learning

◆ Vocal

"Sancta Maria, mater Dei" has a main motive, or **theme** (*a musical idea, usually a melody*) that helps to give balance, symmetry and unity to the piece. Sing the following examples in your own range using solfège syllables. Identify where this theme occurs in the music.

◆ Theory

Review the Vocal section above. Notice that three versions of the theme (examples A, B and D) are based on the **tonic chord,** *a chord built on the home tone, or keynote, of a scale.* In a major scale, the tonic chord is built on the notes *do, mi* and *sol.* Example C of the theme is centered around the key of the **dominant chord,** *a chord built on the fifth note of a scale.* In a major key, this chord uses the notes *sol, ti* and *re.* Music of the Classical period often shifts between the keys of the tonic and dominant chords to provide symmetry and unity.

Evaluation

Demonstrate how well you have learned the skills and concepts featured in the lesson "Sancta Maria, mater Dei" by completing the following:

- In an SATB quartet, perform "Santa Maria, mater Dei." Evaluate your performance based on the small ensemble's ability to sing the homophonic sections with rhythmic precision.

- To evaluate the ability to distinguish the main musical theme of this work from the accompaniment parts, sing the entire piece with the class. Begin by having everyone sitting. As a section sings the theme, that section should stand while singing the theme, and then sit down when they are no longer singing the theme. Evaluate your section's ability to identify and sing the main musical theme of this work.

Sancta Maria, mater Dei, K. 273

For SATB and Piano

Latin Antiphon
Edited by DENIS McCALDIN

WOLFGANG AMADEUS MOZART
(1756–1791)

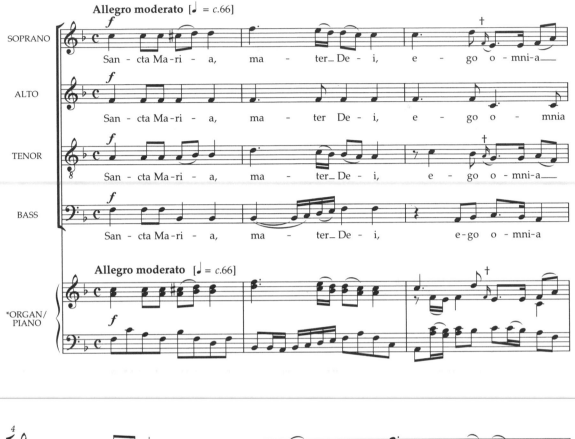

* Mozart's accompaniment is for strings and organ continuo. This organ/piano part follows the string parts and is therefore unfigured.

† ♪♪ †† Before the beat.

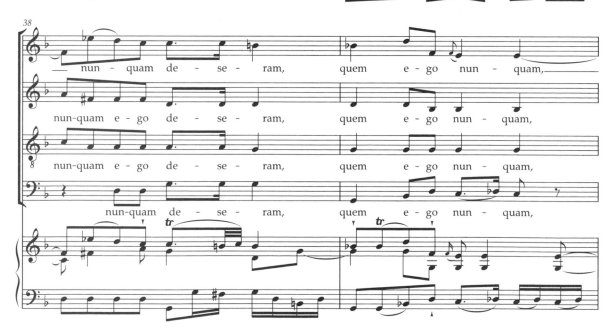

* ♪.

SPOTLIGHT

Arranging

When asked how he approaches choral arranging, composer and arranger Roger Emerson had this to say:

"Generally, an arranger takes the basic melody and accompaniment of a song and prepares it (arranges it) so that it may be performed by a group of instruments or voices. These are things that I take into consideration.

Key

Specifically, as a choral arranger, I begin by finding the best key for the melody. That means finding the scale to use that makes the song the most comfortable to sing. I look for the highest and lowest note of the song, and what ranges would work best for my group of singers.

Melody and Harmony

I then determine the best places for the singers to sing unison or where harmony would be most effective. Using the basic chord symbols as a guide, I like to make the song more interesting by substituting expanded or more colorful chords throughout the song. Depending on the group who will perform the song, I will then write out parts for soprano, alto, tenor and baritone or bass singers, using the melody and new chords that I have chosen.

Accompaniment

The next step is to create a piano accompaniment that supports and hopefully enhances the vocal parts. Particularly in 'pop' style arrangements, the left hand carries a bass line while the right hand plays chords.

Finishing the Arrangement

The final step is to add lyrics, dynamic and style markings.

There are books that provide guidelines for arranging such as chord voicings and comfortable ranges for each instrument or voice, but most 'arrangers' will tell you (like the commercial says) JUST DO IT! Then listen to the outcome and see if you like the way it sounds. We all began somewhere. Good luck!"

Contemporary composer Roger Emerson has over 500 titles in print and 15 million copies in circulation. He is one of the most widely performed choral composers in America today. After a twelve-year teaching career, he now devotes himself full-time to composing, arranging and consulting.

Zigeunerleben

Composer: Robert Schumann (1810–1856)
Text: Emanuel Geibel, English text by Alicia S. Carpenter
Voicing: SATB

VOCABULARY

Romantic period

program music

lied

harmonic minor
  scale

word painting

Focus

- Perform expressively using precise German diction and a full, resonant tone.

- Demonstrate an understanding of word painting and interpretation of the text.

- Perform music representing the Romantic period.

Getting Started

German Romantic composers were fascinated with Gypsies, a nomadic people of North-Indian origin. "Zigeunerleben" describes a night in a Gypsy camp. After dinner they join in dancing and singing. The party goes well into the night, but at dawn the Gypsies are nowhere to be found, having mysteriously disappeared. "Zigeunerleben" was written during the **Romantic period** *(1820–1900)* of Western musical history. Characteristics of the period found in this piece include a wider use of dynamic and expression marks, and a greater interest in melody and tone color rather than harmony and form. "Zigeunerleben" is an example of **program music** *(a descriptive style of music composed to relate a specific incident, situation or drama).* It uses more dissonance and chromaticism than found in music of the Classical period.

MUSIC & HISTORY

To learn more about the Romantic period, see page 136.

◆ History and Culture

Robert Schumann (1810–1856) began taking piano lessons when he was eight years old, which is late by "virtuoso" standards. He began as a law student but convinced his family that he should become a professional pianist. Later, Schumann became a full-time composer after he injured one of his fingers and was no longer able to play the piano professionally. He is best known for his piano music. During 1840, Schumann wrote in excess of 150 songs, or **lied** *(a song in the German language, generally with a secular text)*, including "Zigeunerleben." He is considered one of the leading composers of German lieder, along with Franz Schubert (1797–1828).

Links to Learning

◆ Vocal

Performing Romantic choral music requires a well-supported, fully resonant singing tone. Sing the following example on the neutral syllable "na" while observing the dynamic markings.

◆ Theory

"Zigeunerleben" is written in the key of E minor and is based on the E **harmonic minor scale** *(a minor scale that uses a raised seventh note,* si, *raised from* sol). Sing the E harmonic minor scale.

◆ Artistic Expression

"Zigeunerleben" is filled with examples of **word painting,** *a technique in which the music reflects the meaning of the words.* For example, at letter B, the text describes campfires. How does the music resemble fire? What expression can you add to your voice to help paint the picture? Can you find other examples of word painting?

Evaluation

Demonstrate how well you have learned the skills and concepts featured in the lesson "Zigeunerleben" by completing the following:

- In an octet, perform a section of the piece. Evaluate your ability to sing with a full and resonant tone production.

- Create movements to help express the story of "Zigeunerleben." Evaluate your ability to sing expressively and interpret the meaning of the text through movement.

Zigeunerleben

(Gypsy Life)
Op. 29, No. 8

For SATB and Piano

English text by
ALICIA S. CARPENTER

Words by EMANUEL GEIBEL
Music by ROBERT SCHUMANN (1810–1856)

fül - len ge - schäf - tig den al - ten Po - kal.
fill - ing the gob - lets with wine as they kneel.

fül - len ge - schäf - tig den al - ten Po - kal.
fill - ing the gob - lets with wine as they kneel.

Und Sa - gen und_ Lie - der er - tö - nen im_ Rund, wie
Then songs and old_ leg - ends they sing in the_ night, of

Und Sa - gen und_ Lie - der er - tö - nen im_ Rund, wie
Then songs and old_ leg - ends they sing in the_ night, of

kün-det die Al - te der hor-chen-den Schar.
on to the young once a - gain by the old.

kün-det die Al - te der hor-chen-den Schar.
on to the young once a - gain by the old.

Soprano solo

Schwarz - äu - gi - ge Mäd - chen be - gin-nen den Tanz.
A rav - en-haired maid - en be - gins now to dance,

Alto solo

Da sprü - hen die Fa - ckeln im
And bright as a torch, burns her

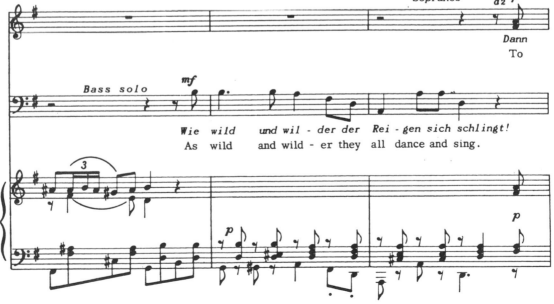

schar-ret das Maul-tier bei Ta-ges-be-ginn, fort ziehn die Ge-stal-ten, wer
shuf-fling of hooves at the break-ing of dawn; They've van-ished, they've van-ished. Who

schar-ret das Maul-tier bei Ta-ges-be-ginn, fort ziehn die Ge-stal-ten, wer
shuf-fling of hooves at the break-ing of dawn; They've van-ished, they've van-ished. Who

sagt dir wo - hin?
knows where they've gone?

Fort
They've

sagt dir wo - hin?
knows where they've gone?

Fort
They've

SPOTLIGHT

Concert Etiquette

A formal musical presentation is a special event that involves many hours of preparation on the part of the individual performers. The ultimate goal of the performers is to put forth their best efforts so that the audience will enjoy and appreciate their talents.

Each performer, whether a singer, instrumentalist, actor, or dancer, must come to the concert totally prepared for his or her individual part. Individual members of an ensemble must be prepared with their own parts, and know how their roles fit into the overall performance picture. Performers should engage their audience by showing enthusiasm and professionalism in every performance. There are no unimportant performances, and each should be viewed as a "really big show."

The manner in which an audience member shows respect and appreciation for the performers is dictated by the particular event. A choir or orchestra concert, a theatre production or a ballet are all formal concerts. As such they dictate specific audience behavior.

In a formal concert setting, the audience is expected to arrive on time and remain quiet and still throughout the entire performance. If a personal emergency does occur during the performance, one should wait to exit the hall when there is a break between the musical selections. Performers love applause and expect the audience to applaud at the end of a musical selection, or when the conductor's hands are lowered. Audience participation should occur when cued by the conductor or performers. No one, including the audience and performers, wants to hear a cellular phone ring during a concert. So, leave the phone turned off and talk later!

Understanding and observing appropriate concert etiquette will ensure that everyone attending the formal music concert enjoys the performance.

Music & History

Links to Music

Renaissance Period **124**

   Il est bel et bon **72**

Baroque Period **128**

   Domine Fili Unigenite **82**

Classical Period **132**

   Sancta Maria, mater Dei, K. 273 . . . . **94**

Romantic Period **136**

   Zigeunerleben **106**

Contemporary Period **140**

   Lux Aurumque **50**

 **MUSIC&ART**

By 1500, Rome was the leading Renaissance city. The popes and the cardinals living in Rome's Vatican made up the wealthiest and most powerful class. They commissioned architects to construct ornate churches and palaces. They had artists create magnificent paintings, like the one above, and sculptures to decorate these buildings. *The School of Athens* is a fresco created by Raphael (1429–1507) for the Stanza della Segnatura (the room where the Pope signed acts of grace) in the Palazzi Pontifici, Vatican, Rome, Italy.

Raphael. *The School of Athens.* c. 1509–11. Stanza della Segnatura, Vatican Palace, Rome, Italy.

Focus

- Describe the Renaissance period, including important developments.
- Identify the distinguishing characteristics and forms of Renaissance music.

The Renaissance— A Time of Exploration

Early in the fifteenth century, a "rebirth" began in Europe— a renewal of creative artistic and musical activity, of intellectual curiosity, of scientific development, and of geographic exploration. This was the beginning of the **Renaissance period (1430–1600),** a period that takes its name from the French word *renaistre,* meaning "to be born again."

For the first time, European sailing ships reached the southern coast of Africa, the Americas, and India, and even succeeded in sailing around the world. These journeys brought an expanding sense of the world, an influx of fresh ideas, and new opportunities for trade. A new merchant class was created, expanding wealth beyond the church and nobility.

Inventions such as the compass and accurate mapping aided exploration, but the most important invention was the printing press with movable type. Knowledge was instantly more available and less expensive when books and other printed materials could be manufactured by a printing press instead of by hand. Learning to read became an important skill and expanded knowledge and critical thinking to people of all classes.

A movement called the Protestant Reformation began during this time. Leaders such as Martin Luther and John Calvin broke away from the Catholic Church to form their own groups. These groups laid the foundation of many Protestant denominations in existence today.

Some of Western civilization's most prized artistic possessions were created during this period. They include Leonardo da Vinci's *Mona Lisa*, Michelangelo's *David*, the ceiling of the Vatican's Sistine Chapel, as well as the literary works of William Shakespeare.

COMPOSERS

Josquin des Prez
(c. 1450–1521)

Giovanni Pierluigi da Palestrina
(c. 1525–1594)

William Byrd
(1543–1623)

Tomás Luis de Victoria
(c. 1548–1611)

Giovanni Gabrieli
(1553–1612)

Claudio Monteverdi
(1567–1643)

ARTISTS

Sandro Botticelli (1445–1510)

Leonardo da Vinci (1452–1519)

Michelangelo (1475–1564)

Raphael (1483–1520)

El Greco (c. 1541–1614)

Michelangelo Merisi da Caravaggio (1571–1610)

AUTHORS

Nicolo Machiavelli (1460–1527)

Martin Luther (1483–1546)

Miguel de Cervantes (1547–1616)

William Shakespeare (1564–1616)

René Descartes (1569–1650)

VOCABULARY

Renaissance period

polyphony

a cappella

Renaissance Choral Music—
The Golden Age of A Cappella Choral Music

Prior to the Renaissance, the majority of composed music was for liturgical services for the Roman Catholic Church and was sung in Latin as part of the church services. During the Renaissance, there was development of the mass and the motet in the Catholic Church as well as the chorale in Protestant churches. There was a rise in popular music, including the madrigal.

- Characteristics of Renaissance choral music can be considered in terms of texture, melody, rhythm, form and tone quality.
- Renaissance choral compositions used **polyphony,** *a type of music in which there are two or more different melodic lines being sung or played at the same time.*
- Equal melody lines were usually smooth, and were often based on modes. Imitation was used frequently. The melody lines combined to create chords and dissonance.
- Meter and stress as we know them were not introduced into choral music until after the Renaissance period. Renaissance music often lacked a clearly defined beat. Instead, choral works had irregular rhythmic groups dictated by the text. This rhythm often varied among the melodic lines, creating a special challenge for the singers.
- Many pieces were sung **a cappella** *(without instrumental accompaniment),* and instruments, when added, simply doubled the voice parts.
- While women participated in singing madrigals, sacred choral works were performed with men and boys singing all the voice parts. The tone quality for these sacred pieces was generally restrained, with little or no vibrato.

Performance Links

When performing music of the Renaissance period, it is important to apply the following guidelines:

- Sing with clarity and purity of tone.
- Balance the vocal lines with equal importance.
- In polyphonic music, sing the rhythms accurately and with precision.
- When designated by the composer, sing a cappella.

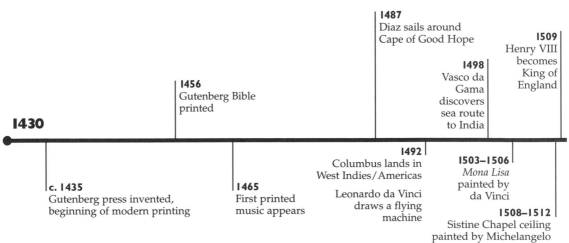

1487
Diaz sails around
Cape of Good Hope

1509
Henry VIII
becomes
King of
England

1498
Vasco da
Gama
discovers
sea route
to India

1456
Gutenberg Bible
printed

1430

1492
Columbus lands in
West Indies / Americas

Leonardo da Vinci
draws a flying
machine

1503–1506
Mona Lisa
painted by
da Vinci

c. 1435
Gutenberg press invented,
beginning of modern printing

1465
First printed
music appears

1508–1512
Sistine Chapel ceiling
painted by Michelangelo

Listening Link
CHORAL SELECTION
L'incoronazione di Poppea, Act III, Scene 8 by Claudio Monteverdi (1567–1643)

Claudio Monteverdi is the most important figure in the transition from Renaissance to Baroque music. While not the first to compose an opera, he was the first to develop opera to its full dramatic and musical potential.

Monteverdi's last opera, *L'incoronazione di Poppea* (in Italian), was written in 1642 when he was 75 years old. It is his greatest musical work. The opera tells the story of people locked in combat for love and power. The setting is imperial Rome, the most powerful nation in the world. The villainous emperor Nero schemes to divorce and banish his wife, Octavia, in favor of his manipulative mistress Poppea.

In the closing scene of the opera depicting a triumph of love over morality, the consuls and tribunes arrive to salute Empress Poppea as she is seated on the throne. A chorus of Tenors and Basses sing with imitation between the two parts. An instrumental interlude then sets the scene for the final love duet between Nero and Poppea.

What is the form of the final duet (ABCA, ABBA, ABAC)? Is dissonance used?

Check Your Understanding

1. List three major nonmusical changes that took place during the Renaissance period.

2. In what ways is *"L'incoronazione di Poppea"* characteristic of the Renaissance period? How is it different?

3. Analyze choral music from the Renaissance and explain how it is different from choral music of today.

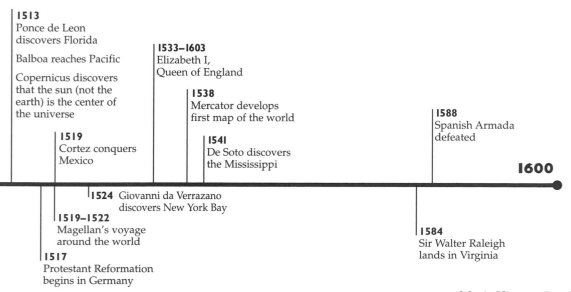

1513
Ponce de Leon discovers Florida

Balboa reaches Pacific

Copernicus discovers that the sun (not the earth) is the center of the universe

1519
Cortez conquers Mexico

1533–1603
Elizabeth I, Queen of England

1538
Mercator develops first map of the world

1541
De Soto discovers the Mississippi

1588
Spanish Armada defeated

1600

1524 Giovanni da Verrazano discovers New York Bay

1519–1522
Magellan's voyage around the world

1517
Protestant Reformation begins in Germany

1584
Sir Walter Raleigh lands in Virginia

Judith Leyster (c. 1600–1660) was the first woman to join the "brotherhood" of the Dutch painters' guild. She was born in Haarlem, in what is now the Netherlands. Although she was highly esteemed by her contemporaries, Leyster remained unknown for a long time and her works were either believed lost, or were attributed to Frans Hals. Her favorite subjects were people involved in everyday activities—including playing music. In 1636, Judith married painter Jan Molenaer.

Judith Leyster. *Boy Playing the Flute*. c. 1630–35. Oil on canvas. 73 x 62 cm (28 11/16 x 24 1/2"). National Museum, Stockholm, Sweden.

Focus

- Describe the Baroque period, including important developments of the time.
- Identify the distinguishing characteristics and forms of Baroque choral music.

The Baroque Period— A Time of Elaboration

The balance and restraint of the Renaissance period were followed by the **Baroque period** *(1600–1750),* in which all the arts, including music, architecture, clothing design and the visual arts, became more emotional, dramatic and decorative. The term *baroque* was derived from a French word for "imperfect or irregular pearls," which were used quite often as decorations on clothing of this period.

The explorations and scientific developments begun during the Renaissance continued and expanded during this period. European navigators, explorers, traders and settlers traveled to other parts of the world, and the first colonies were established in the Americas and elsewhere. Scientists and scholars such as Galileo Galilei and Sir Isaac Newton used new instruments and new insights to make advancements in their specialized fields of study.

The paintings, sculpture and architecture of the Baroque period reflected society's interests in flamboyance, emotional effects and dramatic detail. Elaborate palaces such as Versailles built by King Louis XIV of France were typical of the artistic standards of this period. Such palaces were surrounded by vast formal gardens and decorated with large-scale dramatic paintings and sculptures. The arts were very important, as they were used to display the wealth and splendor of European emperors, kings and other powerful aristocrats.

COMPOSERS

Johann Pachelbel
(1653–1706)

Henry Purcell
(1659–1695)

Antonio Vivaldi
(1678–1741)

Johann Sebastian Bach
(1685–1750)

George Frideric Handel
(1685–1759)

ARTISTS

Peter Paul Rubens
(1577–1640)

Anthony van Dyck
(1599–1641)

Rembrandt van Rijn
(1606–1669)

Judith Leyster
(1609–1660)

Jan Vermeer
(1632–1675)

AUTHORS

John Milton
(1608–1674)

Molière
(1622–1673)

Daniel Defoe
(1660–1731)

Jonathan Swift
(1667–1745)

Samuel Johnson
(1709–1784)

VOCABULARY

Baroque period

improvisation

terraced dynamics

fugue

Baroque Choral Music

Baroque music is described by words such as *splendor, elaboration, theatricality* and *emotionalism.* Characteristics of Baroque choral music can be considered in terms of mood, forms, melody, rhythm, texture and dynamics.

- Baroque compositions tended to project a single mood, or expression of feeling.
- Opera, oratorio, cantata, chorale, motet and mass were the important choral music forms of this period. Instrumentation became more important in choral works. Rather than simply doubling the voices, instruments began to truly provide accompaniments.
- Melody lines were a continuous spinning out of a single melodic idea, often ornamented through **improvisation** *(the art of singing or playing music, making it up as you go).*
- Metered music was introduced. Music was organized and notated in regular groups of beats. The accent within these groups came at regular intervals. The tempo was generally moderate. A steady, unflagging rhythm is considered a major characteristic in choral works of the time. By the end of the seventeenth century, the Italian words used to indicate tempo at the beginning of a piece *(largo, allegro,* and *presto,* for example) had come into general use.
- **Terraced dynamics**—*sudden and abrupt dynamic changes between loud and soft*—were most common and were usually accomplished by increasing or decreasing the number of voices singing.

Performance Links

When performing music of the Baroque period, it is important to apply the following guidelines:

- Sing with pitch accuracy, especially in chromatic sections.
- Be conscious of who has the dominant theme.
- Keep a steady, unrelenting pulse in most pieces. Precision of dotted rhythms is especially important.
- When dynamic level changes occur, all vocal lines need to change together (terraced, contrasting dynamics).

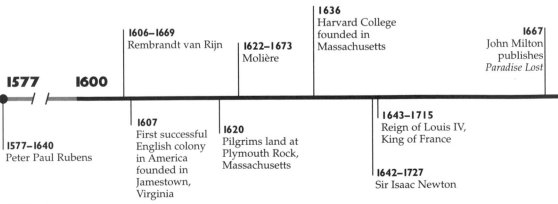

1577   1600

1606–1669
Rembrandt van Rijn

1622–1673
Molière

1636
Harvard College
founded in
Massachusetts

1667
John Milton
publishes
Paradise Lost

1577–1640
Peter Paul Rubens

1607
First successful
English colony
in America
founded in
Jamestown,
Virginia

1620
Pilgrims land at
Plymouth Rock,
Massachusetts

1643–1715
Reign of Louis IV,
King of France

1642–1727
Sir Isaac Newton

Listening Link

CHORAL SELECTION

"Kyrie Eleison" from *Mass in B Minor* by Johann Sebastian Bach (1685–1750)

Bach was born in Eisenach, Germany, and is considered to be one of the best composers of all time. The "Kyrie Eleison" was written in 1733, but the entire *Mass in B Minor* was not completed until 1748. Although different sections were performed at various times, the *Mass in B Minor* was not performed in its entirety until the nineteenth century.

The opening movement begins with a four-bar prelude that sounds like a prayer. The rising Soprano line *Kyrie eleison* means "Lord, have mercy upon us." After an instrumental interlude that features flute and oboe in a **fugue** (*a musical form in which the same melody is performed by different instruments or voices entering at differing times, thus adding layers of sound*), the five vocal parts come in one after another with the same fugal theme. This movement is an excellent example of balance between voices and instruments, as strings and bassoon double the vocal Bass parts while the upper voices are doubled by flutes and oboes in unison or by strings, or, at climactic points, by both strings and woodwinds.

Decide whether or not the entire movement has a polyphonic texture. Identify and list the five voice parts in the order they enter during the fugue.

Check Your Understanding

1. Identify three important nonmusical developments that took place during the Baroque period.

2. Describe the importance of the development of metered music.

3. Analyze choral music from the Baroque period and show how it is different from choral music of the Renaissance.

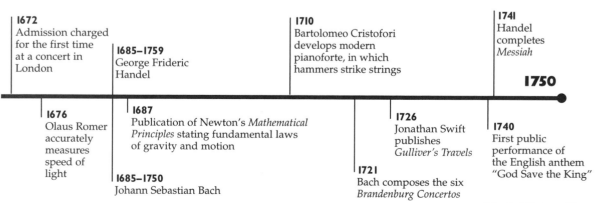

1672
Admission charged for the first time at a concert in London

1685–1759
George Frideric Handel

1710
Bartolomeo Cristofori develops modern pianoforte, in which hammers strike strings

1741
Handel completes *Messiah*

1750

1676
Olaus Romer accurately measures speed of light

1687
Publication of Newton's *Mathematical Principles* stating fundamental laws of gravity and motion

1685–1750
Johann Sebastian Bach

1726
Jonathan Swift publishes *Gulliver's Travels*

1721
Bach composes the six *Brandenburg Concertos*

1740
First public performance of the English anthem "God Save the King"

MUSIC&ART

Thomas Gainsborough (1727–1788) is one of Britain's greatest artists and one of the masters of the eighteenth century. In *Portrait of Miss Ann Ford*, Gainsborough employed a highly unusual pose to convey the unconventional character of a young woman who braved scandal by performing as a professional musician. Miss Ford's informal, twisted pose with her legs crossed was considered a masculine pose and unheard of for ladies. Gainsborough had a keen eye for fashion and was able to capture the shimmering appearance of the sitter's costume.

Thomas Gainsborough. *Portrait of Miss Ann Ford, Later Mrs. Philip Thicknesse.* 1760. Oil on Canvas. 197.2 x 134.9 cm (77 5/8 x 53 1/8"). Cincinnati Art Museum, Cincinnati, Ohio. Bequest of Mary M. Emery.

Focus

- Describe the Classical period, including important developments of the time.
- Identify the distinguishing characteristics and forms of Classical choral music.

The Classical Period— The Age of Enlightenment

The **Classical period** *(1750–1820)* is often called "The Age of Enlightenment." The philosophers and scientists of this era sought the "light" of truth by putting their faith in reason and thought, not in tradition and emotion. This focus on reason resulted in political upheaval and a return to more restrained, less emotional artistic expression. The most important political events of the Classical period brought major changes to specific countries and affected the attitudes and ideas of people in other parts of Europe and the Americas. The American colonists revolted against their British rulers and succeeded in founding the United States of America. Several years later, the French Revolution began; this uprising established a new government and confirmed a new societal structure in France.

The visual artists of the Classical period emulated the balance and grandeur they saw in the surviving works from ancient Greece and Rome. This influence can be seen directly in the subjects chosen by the painters and sculptors of the time. The architecture of the period also reflected these influences. For example, Roman elements can be seen in structures of the time, such as the Brandenburg Gate in Berlin, and Monticello, Thomas Jefferson's home in Virginia.

Scientific discoveries and engineering inventions of this time paved the way for the Industrial Revolution in the Romantic period. Preparation of cotton for cloth production was advanced by the invention of the cotton gin, production of textiles was mechanized, and the invention of the steam engine led to new, more reliable methods of transportation.

COMPOSERS

Christoph Gluck
(1714–1787)

Carl Philipp Emanuel Bach
(1714–1788)

Johann Christian Bach
(1735–1762)

Franz Joseph Haydn
(1732–1809)

Wolfgang Amadeus Mozart
(1756–1791)

ARTISTS

Pietro Longhi
(1702–1788)

Thomas Gainsborough
(1727–1788)

Francisco Goya
(1746–1828)

Jacques-Louis David
(1748–1825)

AUTHORS

Voltaire
(1694–1778)

Jean Jacques Rousseau
(1712–1778)

Johann Wolfgang von Goethe
(1749–1832)

William Wordsworth
(1770–1850)

Jane Austen
(1775–1817)

VOCABULARY

Classical period

homophony

crescendo

decrescendo

Choral Music of the Classical Period

Like other compositions of the time, the choral works reflected the characteristics of the Classical period. These characteristics were reflected in the forms, melody, rhythm, texture, tempo, dynamics and expressive aspects.

- Classical choral music had clearly defined structures with emphasis on symmetry, balance, clarity and restraint.
- Melodies in Classical choral music were often built on chord tones. The texture used was **homophony,** *a single melody with chordal accompaniment*—usually short, clearly defined statements with clear key relationships. Symmetrical phrases with clear cadences were often used.
- An important characteristic of the rhythm in Classical choral compositions was a definite sense of meter. These works generally had a clear steady beat, but it was more relaxed, not the driving force that was often heard in Baroque music.
- While the texture of most Classical choral music was homophonic, fugal or imitative sections were often featured in works of this period.
- Classical choral works usually exhibited a moderate tempo, free from any extremes.
- Gradual crescendos and decrescendos replaced the terraced dynamics of the Baroque period.
- Music ornamentation continued to be featured in choral music, although it was more refined and restrained than in works of the late Baroque. Many choral works included emotional content, but the emotion was expressed less dramatically and with greater detachment than works from the Baroque.

Performance Links

When performing music of the Classical period, it is important to apply the following guidelines:

- Listen for the melody line so the accompaniment parts do not overshadow it.
- Sing chords in tune.
- Make dynamic level changes that move smoothly through **crescendos** (*a dynamic marking used to indicate to gradually become louder*) and **decrescendos** (*a dynamic marking used to indicate to gradually become softer*).
- Keep phrases flowing and connected.

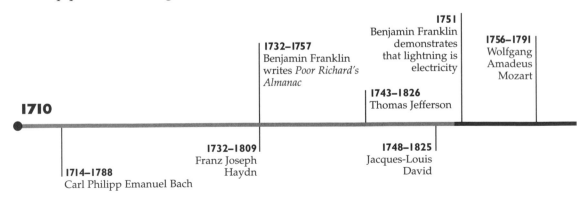

1710

1714–1788
Carl Philipp Emanuel Bach

1732–1809
Franz Joseph
Haydn

1732–1757
Benjamin Franklin
writes *Poor Richard's
Almanac*

1751
Benjamin Franklin
demonstrates
that lightning is
electricity

1743–1826
Thomas Jefferson

1748–1825
Jacques-Louis
David

1756–1791
Wolfgang
Amadeus
Mozart

Listening Links

CHORAL SELECTION

"Laudate Dominum" from *Vesperae solemnes de confessore, K. 339* by Wolfgang Amadeus Mozart (1756–1791)

Born in Salzburg, Austria, on January 27, 1756, Wolfgang Amadeus Mozart is known for his many compositions in virtually every performance medium, from concerto to opera to symphony. He was an amazingly gifted child, and from the age of five, he began to write music of such quality that it astounded the adults around him. As with many gifted individuals, Mozart was misunderstood and did not always receive the recognition he deserved while he was alive. He was alternately world-famous and ignored, all in the course of his too short life. Mozart is ranked alongside Bach and Beethoven as one of the greatest composers ever to have lived.

Vesperae solemnes de confessore dates from 1780 during a period in Mozart's life when, as court organist at Salzburg, he was required to provide music for church services at the Salzburg Cathedral as well as for the local royalty. Mozart apparently enjoyed composing music for religious occasions, as it provided a means to present his music to a wide audience. The text of *Vesperae solemnes de confessore* is based on five psalms. The "Laudate Dominum" is considered one of Mozart's most extraordinary achievements, and it is often performed separately. In this piece, you will hear a beautiful melody, first sung as a solo, then performed in homophonic texture by the choir. Describe the ornamentation used throughout this piece.

Check Your Understanding

1. Identify three important nonmusical developments that took place during the Classical period.

2. Describe the meter, tempo, dynamics, texture and expressive aspects of Mozart's "Laudate Dominum."

3. Analyze how choral music from the Classical period is different from choral music of the Baroque period.

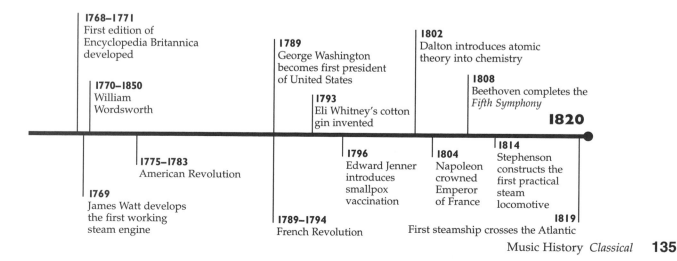

1768–1771
First edition of Encyclopedia Britannica developed

1770–1850
William Wordsworth

1789
George Washington becomes first president of United States

1793
Eli Whitney's cotton gin invented

1802
Dalton introduces atomic theory into chemistry

1808
Beethoven completes the *Fifth Symphony*

1820

1775–1783
American Revolution

1769
James Watt develops the first working steam engine

1796
Edward Jenner introduces smallpox vaccination

1789–1794
French Revolution

1804
Napoleon crowned Emperor of France

1814
Stephenson constructs the first practical steam locomotive

1819
First steamship crosses the Atlantic

 MUSIC & ART

Nineteenth-century musicians often performed for one another in salons. Here, Franz Liszt plays the piano as his friends listen. From left to right are Alexandre Dumas, Victor Hugo, George Sand, Niccolo Paganini, Gioacchino Rossini, and Mademoisellle d'Agoult. In the background are a bust of Beethoven and a portrait of Lord Byron.

Joseph Danhauser. *Liszt at the Piano*. 1840. Oil on canvas. 48.2 x 36.0 cm (19 x 14 1/4"). Nationalgalerie, Berlin, Germany.

Focus

- Describe the Romantic period, including important developments of the time.
- Identify the distinguishing characteristics and forms of Romantic choral music.

The Romantic Period— A Time of Drama

The Classical period had been a time of rules and restraint. Not surprisingly, it was followed by a period of revolt and change. The **Romantic period** *(1820–1900)*, in contrast, was a time of more radical kinds of expression, full of emotion. A new sense of political and artistic freedom emerged during the nineteenth century. The period was characterized by the ideals of liberty and individualism, of dramatic thought and action.

The Romantic period was also a time of tremendous change and modernization in the world—an era that is now called the Industrial Revolution. Scientific and mechanical achievements led to advances in transportation (steamboats, railways), communication (telegraph, telephone), and manufacturing (steel production, food canning). Many nonagricultural jobs came into being, causing a migration from farms and small villages to cities.

The Industrial Revolution also brought about an active and viable middle class that wanted access to the arts. Music and drama "went public," and halls for public viewing proliferated. It was also a time of important social change as slavery was outlawed in England and later in the United States.

Artists of the Romantic period began to explore the world around them rather than portray scenes from religion or famous stories and myths. They began to paint from nature and explore the role of natural light on the scenes they observed. Those in France were called Impressionists and included the artists Manet, Degas and Renoir, and the sculptor Rodin.

COMPOSERS

Ludwig van Beethoven (1770–1827)

Gioacchino Rossini (1792–1868)

Franz Schubert (1797–1828)

Frédéric Chopin (1810–1849)

Franz Liszt (1811–1886)

Richard Wagner (1813–1883)

Stephen Foster (1826–1864)

Johannes Brahms (1833–1897)

Peter Ilyich Tchaikovsky (1840–1893)

ARTISTS

Joseph Danhauser (1805–1845)

James Whistler (1834–1903)

Paul Cezanne (1839–1906)

Claude Monet (1840–1926)

Pierre-Auguste Renoir (1841–1919)

Mary Cassatt (1845–1926)

Vincent van Gogh (1853–1890)

Harry O. Tanner (1859–1903)

AUTHORS

Victor Hugo (1802–1885)

George Sand (1804–1876)

Henry Wadsworth Longfellow (1807–1882)

Harriet Beecher Stowe (1811–1896)

Charles Dickens (1812–1870)

Leo Tolstoy (1828–1910)

Mark Twain (1835–1910)

Rudyard Kipling (1865–1905)

VOCABULARY

Romantic period

art song

grand opera

operetta

vibrato

Romantic Choral Music

During the Romantic period, composers created music that was often exaggerated and burst forth with emotion. It was, in many ways, a reaction against the Classical period, when music was based on emotional restraint and formal structure. The flamboyance of these works was expressed in their forms, melodies, rhythms, tempos, dynamics, textures, harmonies, expressive aspects and tone qualities.

- Romantic choral music forms included **grand opera** (*a large-scale opera that is sung throughout, without spoken dialogue*), **operetta** (*a light opera, often with spoken dialogue and dancing*), and **art songs** (*expressive songs about life, love, and human relationships, usually for solo voice and piano*).
- Melodies in romantic choral works were long and lyrical. Irregular phrase lengths were often used. Wide angular skips and extreme, unpredictable contrasts led to big climaxes.
- Composers made use of frequent changes in meter to add interest. Exotic and nationalistic rhythmic characteristics were featured.
- Crescendos and decrescendos were widely and expressively used.
- The texture was often thick, with an emphasis on rich sound. Most works emphasized homophony rather than polyphony.
- Individual and personal emotions were given free expression, and unusual harmonic, rhythmic and dynamic effects were frequently used.
- **Vibrato,** *a fluctuation of pitch on a single note,* was used to add warmth to the tone quality. In general, fullness of tone was emphasized and beauty of tone was considered essential.

Performance Links

When performing music of the Romantic period, it is important to apply the following guidelines:

- Understand the relation of the text to the melody and harmony.
- Concentrate on phrasing, and maintain a clear, beautiful melodic line.
- Perform accurately the wide range of dynamics and tempos.
- Sing confidently in foreign languages to reflect nationalism in music.

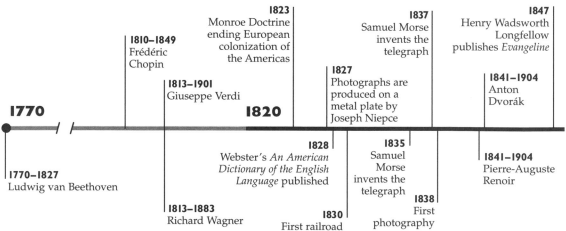

Listening Link

CHORAL SELECTION

Symphony #9 in D Minor ("Choral"), Fourth Movement (Finale) by Ludwig van Beethoven (1770–1827)

Ludwig van Beethoven, one of our greatest composers, was born in the small town of Bonn, Germany. At age 38, he experienced a great tragedy—he went completely deaf. *Symphony #9 in D Minor* was the last major piece Beethoven wrote. Beethoven wrote nine symphonies, eleven overtures, incidental music to plays, a violin concerto and five piano concertos, sixteen string quartets, nine piano trios and other chamber music, ten violin sonatas and five violoncello sonatas, thirty large piano sonatas and more. It is said that Beethoven wrote music with great difficulty and that he labored over each note. Beethoven's music is often seen as an outpouring of his personality. It is often emotional and exuberant, but at other times it may express tenderness or sadness.

The finale of the Fourth Movement of the *Symphony #9 in D Minor* is a setting for soloists and chorus of Friedrich Schiller's poem "Ode to Joy." Beethoven chose the stanzas that emphasize two ideas—the universal brotherhood of man through joy, and the love of an eternal heavenly Father. This section of the Fourth Movement is a fascinating interplay between soloists, quartets, full choir, duets, trios and orchestral interludes. Try to map out what you hear as you listen to this dramatic work. Listen a second time and focus on the orchestral accompaniment throughout the piece. Finally, try to envision composing all these complex rhythms and melodies while forced to live in total silence.

Check Your Understanding

1. Identify three important nonmusical developments that took place during the Romantic period.

2. In what ways is "Ode to Joy" characteristic of the Romantic period?

3. Analyze music from the Romantic period and explain how it is different from music of the Classical period.

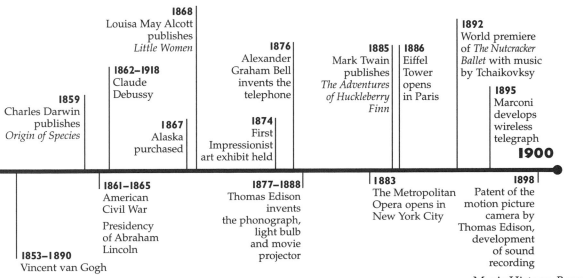

1859 Charles Darwin publishes *Origin of Species*

1868 Louisa May Alcott publishes *Little Women*

1862–1918 Claude Debussy

1867 Alaska purchased

1876 Alexander Graham Bell invents the telephone

1874 First Impressionist art exhibit held

1885 Mark Twain publishes *The Adventures of Huckleberry Finn*

1886 Eiffel Tower opens in Paris

1892 World premiere of *The Nutcracker Ballet* with music by Tchaikovksy

1895 Marconi develops wireless telegraph

1900

1853–1890 Vincent van Gogh

1861–1865 American Civil War / Presidency of Abraham Lincoln

1877–1888 Thomas Edison invents the phonograph, light bulb and movie projector

1883 The Metropolitan Opera opens in New York City

1898 Patent of the motion picture camera by Thomas Edison, development of sound recording

Fernando Botero (b. 1932), a Colombian painter, illustrator and sculptor, began working as an illustrator in 1948. In his work, Botero exaggerates the proportions of the human figure. This has become a highly recognizable characteristic of his work. In *Dancing in Colombia,* Botero uses line, color, shape, form, emphasis, proportion and balance to create movement and rhythm in his painting.

Fernando Botero. *Dancing in Colombia.* 1980. Oil on canvas. 188 x 231.1 cm (74 x 91"). The Metropolitan Museum of Art, New York, New York. Anonymous Gift, 1983.

Focus

- Describe the Contemporary period, including important developments of the time.
- Identify the distinguishing characteristics and forms of Contemporary choral music.

The Contemporary Period— The Search for Originality

Change, experimentation, innovation, and exploration— these have been the central features of life during the Contemporary period, the time from 1900 until right now. A thirst for knowledge and adventure has led to many major discoveries that have revealed ancient human life on Earth, and exploration of our moon, other planets, and the highest and lowest points on Earth. Some of these discoveries include:

1922—British archaeologist Howard Carter opens the tomb of Tutankhamen, an Egyptian pharaoh who died in 1325 B.C.

1940—French children, looking for their dog, come across the Lascaux Cave, whose walls are decorated with paintings dating from the Ice Age.

1953—Mount Everest is scaled by Sir Edmund Hilary and his guide.

1959—Mary Leakey discovers the fossilized skull of a human ancestor who lived 1.8 million years ago in Tanzania.

1960—The bathyscaph *Trieste* carries its crew nearly seven miles into the Mariana trench in the Pacific to the deepest part of the ocean.

1969—American astronauts walk on the moon.

1985—Oceanographers locate the sunken liner *Titanic* in the Atlantic.

2003—Three unmanned spacecraft land on Mars for a close scientific examination to determine the past of this planet.

COMPOSERS

Arnold Schoenberg (1874–1951)

Béla Bartók (1881–1945)

Igor Stravinsky (1882–1971)

Heitor Villa-Lobos (1887–1959)

William Grant Still (1895–1978)

Francis Poulenc (1899–1963)

Aaron Copland (1900–1990)

Benjamin Britten (1913–1976)

ARTISTS

Pablo Picasso (1881–1973)

Diego Rivera (1886–1957)

Georgia O'Keeffe (1887–1986)

Jacob Lawrence (1917–2000)

Andrew Wyeth (b. 1917)

Fernando Botero (b. 1932)

AUTHORS

Robert Frost (1874–1963)

Virginia Woolf (1882–1941)

Ernest Hemingway (1899–1961)

James Baldwin (1924–1997)

Gabriel García Márquez (b. 1928)

VOCABULARY

Contemporary period

expressionism

neo-classicism

New Romanticism

avant-garde

Choral Music of the Contemporary Period

The **Contemporary period** *(1900–present)* is made up of many diverse musical styles in both choral and instrumental music. Some of these musical styles are built on previous traditions, while others explore new sounds and structures. While no one statement can fully characterize the music of this period, it is possible to consider four major trends:

Expressionism—*music of the early twentieth century, usually associated with Germany, that was written in a deeply subjective and introspective style.*

Neo-Classicism—*music of the early twentieth century characterized by the inclusion of contemporary styles or features derived from the music of the seventeenth and eighteenth centuries.*

New Romanticism—*a genuine tonal melody composed with exotic texture and timbres.*

Avant-Garde—*a term used in the arts to denote those who make a radical departure from tradition.*

Melody: Expressionism—tone rows and serialism, angular and irregular melodies
              Neo-Classicism—diatonic, angular melodies
              New Romanticism—warm, lyric melodies
              Avant-Garde—fragmented or nonexistent melodies, new sounds used

Rhythm: Expressionism—rhythmic motives present; influence of jazz can be heard
              Neo-Classicism—strong sense of meter, syncopation and driving rhythms
              New Romanticism—use of various tempos to emphasize changes in mood
              Avant-Garde—rhythm sometimes complex, sometimes irrelevant

Dynamics: Expressionism—full range of dynamics
              Neo-Classicism—restrained, rapid changes and strong accents
              New Romanticism—full range of dynamics, not extreme
              Avant-Garde—anything goes

Performance Links

When performing music of the Contemporary period, it is important to apply the following guidelines:

- Sing on pitch, even in extreme parts of your range.
- Tune intervals carefully in the skips found in many melodic lines.
- Sing changing meters and unusual rhythm patterns precisely.
- Perform accurately the wide range in dynamics and tempos.

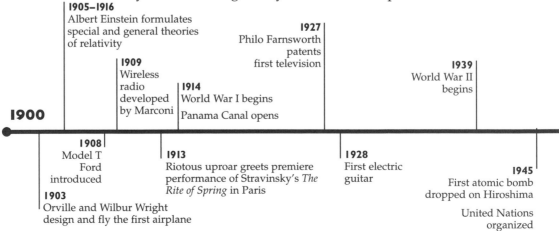

1905–1916 Albert Einstein formulates special and general theories of relativity

1927 Philo Farnsworth patents first television

1909 Wireless radio developed by Marconi

1914 World War I begins / Panama Canal opens

1939 World War II begins

1900

1908 Model T Ford introduced

1913 Riotous uproar greets premiere performance of Stravinsky's *The Rite of Spring* in Paris

1928 First electric guitar

1945 First atomic bomb dropped on Hiroshima / United Nations organized

1903 Orville and Wilbur Wright design and fly the first airplane

Listening Link
CHORAL SELECTION
Requiem: Sanctus by Maurice Duruflé (1902–1986)

Maurice Duruflé was born in Louviers, France, but spent most of his life in Paris. He studied the piano and organ throughout his life, and was a respected composer and distinguished organist. He won many awards for composition, organ and harmony during his career, and made two separate performance tours of the United States in the 1960s. He was also a professor of music theory and the director of the Gregorian Institute at the Paris Conservatory. He composed only fourteen pieces throughout his career.

Duruflé 's greatest and most performed work is his *Requiem, Op. 9* for Soprano, Baritone, chorus, organ, and orchestra, written in 1947. At the time it was commissioned by a French publishing company, Duruflé was composing a suite for organ solo based on the Gregorian chants of the mass for the dead, or requiem. It was this suite that was expanded and transformed to become Duruflé's setting of the requiem. The result was the composer's first choral work. It is one of the best-known requiems of the twentieth century.

Duruflé wrote very few melodies for his *Requiem,* but instead used the medieval Gregorian chants in a typically twentieth-century harmonic and orchestral setting. In the composer's own words, "I … have tried to reconcile, as far as possible, the very flexible Gregorian rhythms as established by the Benedictines of Solesmes with … modern notation." He preserved the fluid and improvisatory qualities of these beautiful chants.

The "Sanctus" is the fourth section of the *Requiem.* The English translation of the Latin text is "Holy, holy, holy, Lord God of Sabaoth! Heaven and earth are full of your glory. Hosanna in the highest!" What text is used at the climax of this piece? Describe the dynamic plan used by the composer.

Check Your Understanding

1. Identify three important nonmusical developments that took place during the Contemporary period.

2. What characteristics of the Contemporary period are heard in "Sanctus" from *Requiem* by Maurice Duruflé? What Contemporary period trend does the work suggest?

3. Analyze music from the Contemporary period and explain how it is different from music of the Classical period.

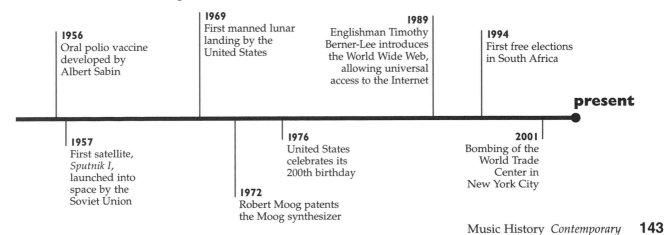

1956
Oral polio vaccine developed by Albert Sabin

1969
First manned lunar landing by the United States

1989
Englishman Timothy Berner-Lee introduces the World Wide Web, allowing universal access to the Internet

1994
First free elections in South Africa

present

1957
First satellite, *Sputnik I,* launched into space by the Soviet Union

1972
Robert Moog patents the Moog synthesizer

1976
United States celebrates its 200th birthday

2001
Bombing of the World Trade Center in New York City

SPOTLIGHT

Musical Theater

Tim McDonald, the current creative director of Music Theatre International in New York City, was asked to share his ideas on musical theater in today's schools. This is what he has to say:

"Musical theater (sometimes spelled theatre) is a uniquely American art form like jazz and rock-and-roll that has become popular all over the world. Recently, musicals have been in the spotlight with major motion picture releases and television specials. Also, performers like Tom Cruise, Britney Spears and Tom Hanks as well as directors Baz Luhrmann and Tim Burton have credited their success to participating in their school's musical.

An annual student musical has become a regular part of the school calendar. In fact, it is estimated that 50,000 productions are presented in school auditoriums and over 2.5 million young people participate in their school musical each year. Most everyone can participate in a student musical on some level. Each person's contribution adds to the success of the production. For those who enjoy singing, dancing or acting, there's probably a role for you or a place in the ensemble. For those who like to be behind the scenes, there's directing, stage managing, choreography and the technical crew. If your interests lean more towards visual art, there are sets to be designed and painted, props to be imagined, and costumes to be crafted.

The best part of participating in a musical is that it's a lot of fun! So the next time you see an audition notice, take a chance and audition or talk to the director about working behind the scenes. Who knows, one day you may credit your school musical with the success of your career."

In 1952, Frank Loesser transformed a fledgling business into what is now known throughout the world as "MTI." Music Theatre International is a theatrical licensing company specializing in Broadway musicals. It has been instrumental in extending the production life of the great American musicals such as, Guys and Dolls, West Side Story, Fiddler On The Roof, Les Misérables, Annie, Of Thee I Sing, Ain't Misbehavin', Damn Yankees, The Music Man, Godspell, Little Shop Of Horrors *and the musical theater collaboration of composer/lyricist Stephen Sondheim, among others.*

Choral Library

America, The Beautiful 146

Ave Maria 158

Dörven Dalai 164

I'm Gonna Sing ''Til The Spirit Moves
In My Heart 172

If Music Be The Food Of Love 186

The Last Words Of David 198

Pingos D'água 208

A Rose Touched By The Sun's Warm Rays . 216

Set Me As A Seal 220

Skylark 226

Somewhere 236

Sorida 246

America, The Beautiful

Composer: Samuel A. Ward, arranged by John Leavitt
Text: Katharine Lee Bates
Voicing: SATB divisi

VOCABULARY
variation
relative minor scale

Focus

- Perform music in major and minor tonality.
- Demonstrate an understanding of variation in music.
- Perform music representing the American heritage.

SPOTLIGHT

To learn more about arranging, see page 105.

Getting Started

Think about all the different ways you have heard "The Star-Spangled Banner" performed. You may have heard it performed by a soloist, a choir, a marching band or a stadium full of people. Although all are performing the same song, each performance sounds different. Composers often take the same melody and create different sounds through the technique of **variation,** *the modifying of a musical idea, usually after its initial appearance in the piece.* In this setting of "America, The Beautiful," the arranger has added variation by shifting the tonality of the song from a major key to a minor key.

◆ History and Culture

Katharine Lee Bates (1859–1929), a psychology professor at Wellesley College in Massachusetts, wrote the poem "America, The Beautiful" after experiencing the view from atop Pike's Peak in the Colorado Rocky Mountains. Her poem first appeared in print in 1895. Originally, the poem was set to several popular melodies of the day, including "Auld Lang Syne." Samuel A. Ward (1847–1903) wrote a song in 1882 called "Materna." In 1910, the words to "America, The Beautiful" were adapted to his melody "Materna." Although some people tried to adopt "America, The Beautiful" as the national anthem, on March 3, 1931, President Herbert Hoover signed a bill making the more established "The Star-Spangled Banner" our official national anthem. Over the years, "America, The Beautiful" has become the country's unofficial second national anthem.

Links to Learning

◆ Vocal

The **relative minor scale** is *a scale that shares the same key signature as its corresponding major scale.* Both scales share the same half steps: between *mi* and *fa*, and *ti* and *do*. Sing the B♭ major scale in your appropriate range.

B♭	C	D	E♭	F	G	A	B♭	A	G	F	E♭	D	C	B♭
do	re	mi	fa	sol	la	ti	do	ti	la	sol	fa	mi	re	do

The relative minor scale uses the same pitches as the major scale, but has *la* as its home tone, or keynote. Sing the G minor scale in your appropriate range.

G	A	B♭	C	D	E♭	F	G	F	E♭	D	C	B♭	A	G
la	ti	do	re	mi	fa	sol	la	sol	fa	mi	re	do	ti	la

◆ Theory

Arranger John Leavitt created a variation of the melody of "America, The Beautiful" in measures 46–61. Compare this melody variation to the original melody found in measures 22–37. What has been changed? Sing both sections on solfège syllables. Do you recognize the use of the relative minor scale? What evidence do you see?

Evaluation

Demonstrate how well you have learned the skills and concepts featured in the lesson "America, The Beautiful" by completing the following:

- With one singer on a part, sing measures 46–61 and measures 22–37 on solfège syllables, then on words. Evaluate how well you were able to sing in tune in both major and minor tonality.

- As a solo, sing "Row, Row, Row Your Boat" in a major key of your choice. Create a variation of the song by changing the rhythm, changing the time signature, altering the melody line slightly, or changing the key from major to its relative minor. Perform your variation for a classmate. Discuss the elements you used to create variation. Analyze how well you were able to demonstrate the concept of variation. Switch roles with your classmate. Evaluate each other's work.

America, The Beautiful

For SATB divisi and Piano

Arranged with additional music by
JOHN LEAVITT

Words by KATHARINE LEE BATES
Music by SAMUEL A. WARD

crown thy good with broth - er - hood From sea to shin - ing

sea!

flaw, _____ Con - firm thy soul in self - con - trol, Thy lib - er - ty in

Unis.

law!

Richly *mf*

O

cresc.

mf

65 (Opt. div.)

Tenor

beau - ti - ful for he - roes proved In lib - er - at - ing strife, Who

Bass

(opt. a cappella through m.79)

more than self their coun-try loved And mer-cy more than life! _____ A-

mer - i - ca! A - mer - i - ca! May God thy gold re - fine _____ Till

all suc-cess be no-ble-ness, And ev-'ry gain di - vine!

(Play)

f

al - a - bas - ter cit - ies gleam, Un -

94 *crisp!*

dimmed by hu - man tears! A - mer - i - ca! A -

crisp!

div.

mer - i - ca! God shed His grace on

Ave Maria

Composer: Javier Busto
Text: Liturgical Latin
Voicing: SATB divisi

VOCABULARY
form
antiphon
diphthong
octet

Focus

- Perform music expressively, using tall, uniform Latin vowels.
- Describe the relationship between text and musical form.
- Analyze ABC form.

Getting Started

When choreographers create a dance, they often choose the music first, and then create the dance to fit the music. The music often dictates the form of the dance. In writing choral music, composers sometimes select the text first, and then allow the text to dictate the **form** (*the structure or design of a musical composition*) of the song. "Ave Maria" is based on the Marian prayer (a prayer to Mary) of the same name. There are three sections to the prayer. As you learn "Ave Maria," look for ways that the text dictates the form of the song (ABC form).

 **SKILL BUILDERS**

To learn more about the key of G major, see Advanced Sight-Singing, *pages 1-11.*

◆ History and Culture

"Ave Maria" ("Hail Mary") is a prayer found in the *Liber Antiphonarius* of St. Gregory the Great (d. 604) as an **antiphon** (*a short verse sung before and after a psalm or canticle*) for the fourth Sunday of Advent, the time just prior to Christmas in the liturgical (church) year. It consists of three sections. The opening section is based on the greeting to Mary by the Angel Gabriel (measures 7–14); the middle section is the greeting of St. Elizabeth to Mary when Mary visited her (measures 15–26); and the final section is based on the petition for intercession (measures 27–43). Composer Javier Busto, who has a degree in medicine, was born in the Basque region of Spain in 1949.

Links to Learning

◆ Vocal

A **diphthong** is *a combination of two vowel sounds.* For example, the vowel "ay" consists of two sounds: "eh" and "ee." Latin vowels are pure vowels, without diphthongs. Sing the following example to practice singing Latin vowels correctly.

	(diphthong)							(diphthong)	
1. (incorrect)	ah veh ee	ma	ree	ah	grah	tsee	ah	pleh ee	nah
2. (correct)	ah vch (pure vowel)	ma	ree	ah	grah	tsee	ah	pleh (pure vowel)	nah

Apply what you have learned to the first section of this piece. Sing measures 7–12 using pure, tall Latin vowels without diphthongs.

◆ Artistic Expression

Search the Internet, ask a Latin teacher, or seek out other references to find a literal translation of this Latin text. Note the textual and musical form of the work, as well as the different moods the three sections evoke. How does Busto vary the compositional style of his writing to express the meaning of the text?

Evaluation

Demonstrate how well you have learned the skills and concepts featured in the lesson "Ave Maria" by completing the following:

- In an **octet** *(eight singers)*, perform "Ave Maria" demonstrating varied dynamics, tall Latin vowels, and accurate pitches and rhythms. Evaluate how well the group did. Rate your performance based on a scale of 1–5, with 5 being the best.

- Identify the three sections of "Ave Maria." On a sheet of paper draw three columns and label each A, B, or C. Under each column, list and describe the musical characteristics of each section, including pitch, rhythm, text, dynamics, tempo and texture. Evaluate how well you were able to analyze ABC form.

Ave Maria

For SATB divisi and Piano or Organ

Liturgical Latin

Music by
JAVIER BUSTO

fru - ctus ven - tris tu - i   Je - sus,   Je - sus,   *f* San - cta Ma - ri - a

fru - ctus ven - tris tu - i   Je - sus,   Je - sus,   *f* San - cta Ma - ri - a

ma - ter   de - i,   o - ra pro no - bis pec - ca - to - ri - bus, o - ra pro no - bis

ma - ter   de - i,   o - ra pro no - bis pec - ca - to - ri - bus, o - ra pro no - bis

O - ra pro no - bis   pec - ca -

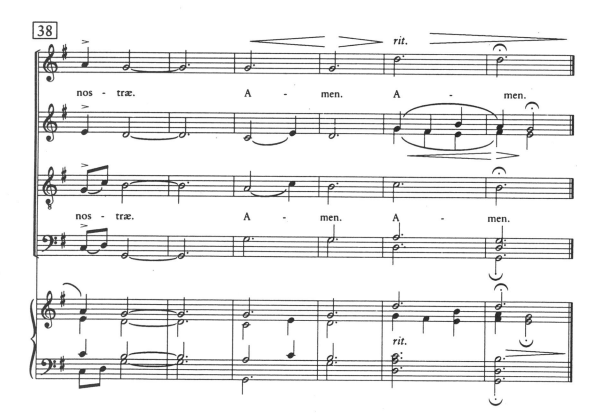

Dörven Dalai

Composer: Inner Mongolian Folk Song, arranged by Yongrub
Text: Inner Mongolian Folk Song
Voicing: SATB

VOCABULARY

articulation

pentatonic scale

Focus

- Perform music demonstrating clear and crisp articulation.
- Read and improvise music using the pentatonic scale.
- Perform music representing Inner Mongolian (Chinese) culture.

Getting Started

The history, traditions and characteristics of a culture are preserved in their music and artistic creations. "Dörven Dalai" is a Chinese welcoming song from Eastern Inner Mongolia. Folk songs are a vital part of life in Mongolia, and it is common to hear the people singing these wonderful melodies, full of legends and fairy tales. "Dörven Dalai" is a song of rejoicing, bringing people together to share the happiness of life. A general translation of the words is as follows:

As clear as the water of the West Sea, as gentle as the areca leaves.
With happiness and good fortune we have met.
Let's raise our cups, rejoice and sing,
And enjoy this happy moment together.

 **SKILL BUILDERS**

To learn more about sixteenth notes see Advanced Sight-Singing, pages 44–45.

◆ History and Culture

When you hear the word *Mongolia*, what comes to mind? Perhaps you have studied the great thirteenth-century emperor Genghis Khan, who with his Mongol army conquered two-thirds of the known world. Can you picture this area of the world? Mongolia is a region in northern China with a population of over 20 million people. Much of Mongolia is a high plateau with a severe climate. While there are a few industrial cities, much of the population lives in rural areas. Mongolia is the largest producer of sheep wool, goat wool and cashmere in China. The arranger of this piece, Yongrub (b. 1934), is a member of the Inner Mongolian Radio Performance Group and writes both choral and symphonic music.

Links to Learning

◆ Vocal

The rhythmic complexities of "Dörven Dalai" require clear, crisp **articulation** *(the amount of separation or connection between notes).* Perform the following example to develop clear and crisp articulation. Change the pitch up or down by half steps on each repeat. Exaggerate the movement of the lips while singing lightly.

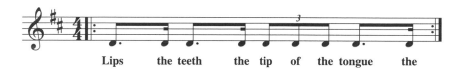

Lips   the teeth   the tip   of   the tongue   the

◆ Theory

The **pentatonic scale** is *a five-tone scale using the pitches* do, re, mi, sol, la. Using the pitches D♯, F♯, G♯, A♯, C♯, D♯, play the pentatonic scale on a keyboard.

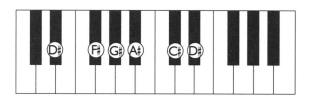

Sing the pentatonic scale in your appropriate range. Can you play the Soprano part in measures 1–7 of "Dörven Dalai" using the same pentatonic scale?

la   do   re   mi   sol   la

Evaluation

Demonstrate how well you have learned the skills and concepts featured in the lesson "Dörven Dalai" by completing the following:

- Sing measures 19–24 (Tenor/Bass) or measures 32–37 (Soprano/Alto) as a duet, with one on each part. Evaluate how well you were able to sing with clear and crisp articulation.

- Perform one of the melodies found in the song on a keyboard, using only the five black keys. Evaluate the accuracy of your performance.

- In an SATB quartet, perform "Dörven Dalai" standing near a piano. As the quartet sings, select a fifth student to improvise a new melody based on the pentatonic scale described above in the Theory section. Take turns playing the improvisation. Do you think the piano improvisations enhance the singing performances? Why or why not?

Dörven Dalai
(The Four Seas)

For SATB, a cappella

Arranged by YONGRUB

Inner Mongolian Folk Song

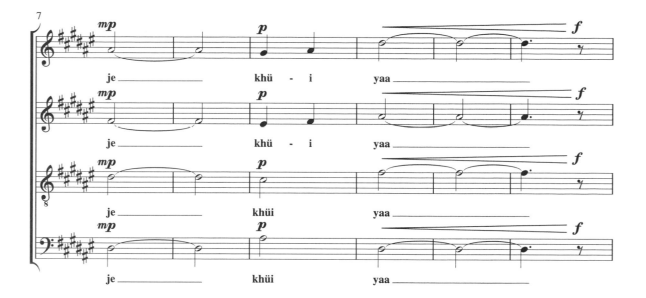

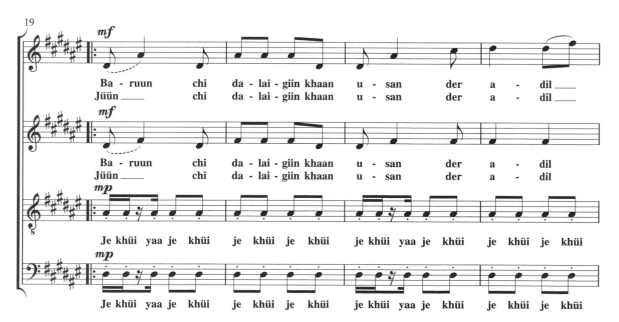

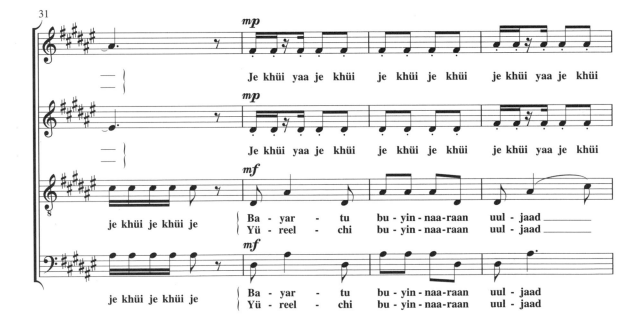

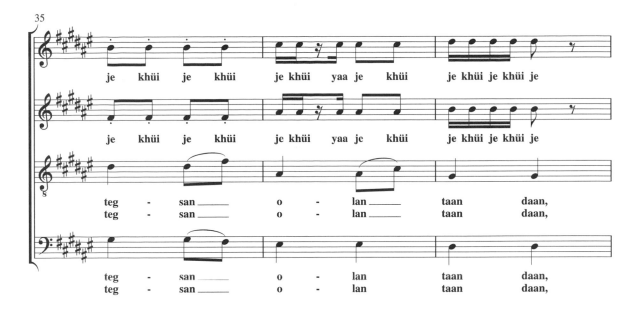

je khüi je khüi je khüi yaa je khüi je khüi je khüi je

je khüi je khüi je khüi yaa je khüi je khüi je khüi je

teg - san ___ o - lan ___ taan daan,
teg - san ___ o - lan ___ taan daan,

teg - san ___ o - lan taan daan,
teg - san ___ o - lan taan daan,

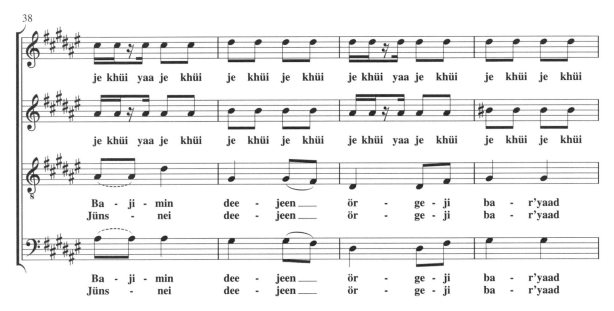

je khüi yaa je khüi je khüi je khüi je khüi yaa je khüi je khüi je khüi

je khüi yaa je khüi je khüi je khüi je khüi yaa je khüi je khüi je khüi

Ba - ji - min dee - jeen ___ ör - ge - ji ba - r'yaad
Jüns - nei dee - jeen ___ ör - ge - ji ba - r'yaad

Ba - ji - min dee - jeen ___ ör - ge - ji ba - r'yaad
Jüns - nei dee - jeen ___ ör - ge - ji ba - r'yaad

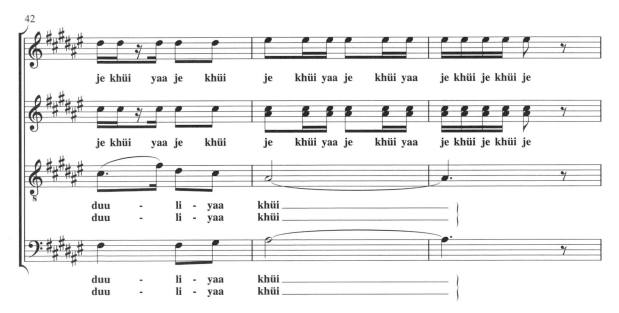

je khüi yaa je khüi je khüi yaa je khüi yaa je khüi je khüi je

je khüi yaa je khüi je khüi yaa je khüi yaa je khüi je khüi je

duu - li - yaa khüi ___
duu - li - yaa khüi ___

duu - li - yaa khüi ___
duu - li - yaa khüi ___

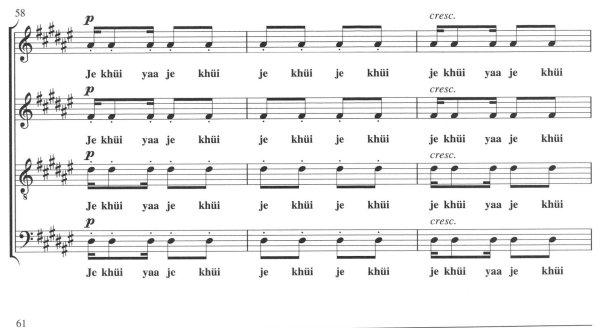

I'm Gonna Sing 'Til The Spirit Moves In My Heart

Composer: Moses Hogan
Text: Moses Hogan
Voicing: SATB divisi

VOCABULARY

spiritual

syncopation

melisma

Focus

- Sing with rhythmic accuracy while maintaining a steady beat.
- Perform music representing the African American spiritual.

Getting Started

How important is music in your life? Could you make it through the day without humming, singing or listening to music? Most cultures around the world include singing as a part of their daily life, working or playing, or as an expression of human emotion. Although "I'm Gonna Sing 'Til The Spirit Moves In My Heart" is an original composition, it is written in the style of an African American **spiritual** *(songs that were first sung by the African American slaves, usually based on biblical themes or stories)*. The use of **syncopation** *(accents on weak beats or on notes that normally do not receive extra emphasis)* and **melismas** *(a group of notes sung to a single syllable or word)* help create the spiritual style. Moses Hogan creatively paints the text of the phrase "Can't you feel the spirit movin'" by layering the vocal parts and using melismas. "I'm Gonna Sing 'Til The Spirit Moves In My Heart" may become an important song in your life because it expresses such happiness and joy!

◆ History and Culture

Moses George Hogan (1957–2003) was a classical pianist, conductor, composer and internationally distinguished arranger of American spirituals. Mr. Hogan was born in New Orleans and studied with jazz pianist Ellis Marsalis. He studied music at Oberlin College and also at the Juilliard School. In the 1990s, Mr. Hogan formed the Moses Hogan Chorale and, later, the Moses Hogan Singers.

SPOTLIGHT

To learn more about improvisation, see page 215.

Links to Learning

◆ **Vocal**

"I'm Gonna Sing 'Til The Spirit Moves In My Heart" is written in the key of F minor. Perform the following example to practice singing the F natural minor scale. Sing in your appropriate range.

Loo   loo loo   loo loo loo loo   loo   loo loo   loo loo loo loo   loo.

◆ **Theory**

While clapping a steady quarter note pulse, chant the following rhythmic pattern, using the rhythm syllables provided. Repeat each pattern until mastered, then, without missing a beat, move on to the next measure.

Syn-co - pa ti   ti ka   (syn) co - pa   ti   ti ka   (syn) co - pa   ti   ti (ka)

In the following example, clap the rhythm and chant the text.

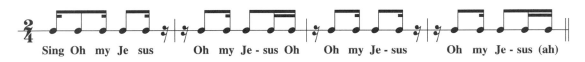

Sing Oh my Je sus   Oh my Je - sus Oh   Oh my Je - sus   Oh my Je - sus (ah)

◆ **Artistic Expression**

Sing measures 10–17 with energy and rhythmic accuracy. Identify the important words. Sing again, stressing the important words more than the others. Experiment with stressing other words. How do the choices you make affect the performance?

Evaluation

Demonstrate how well you have learned the skills and concepts featured in the lesson "I'm Gonna Sing 'Til The Spirit Moves In My Heart" by completing the following:

- As a solo, sing the "small group" section from measures 1–17 with rhythmic accuracy and by observing the accent markings. Evaluate how well you were able to do both. Rate your performance on a scale of 1 to 5, with 5 being the best.

- Videotape yourself with a small ensemble performing a section of "I'm Gonna Sing 'Til The Spirit Moves In My Heart." Review your taped performance with the sound on and then again with the sound off. Evaluate how well you were able to convey the meaning of the text through facial expression and stage presence.

I'm Gonna Sing 'Til The Spirit Moves In My Heart

For SATB divisi, a cappella

Words and Music by
MOSES HOGAN

Pronounced "Je-su-sa."

pray 'til the spi-rit moves___ in my heart. I'm gon-na pray 'til Je - sus comes.___

div.

Oh my Je - sus Oh my Je - sus Oh Oh my Je - sus

Tenor *f* ——— *p*

Can't you feel the spi-rit mov - in'___

Bass *mp*

Can't you feel it

f ——— *p*

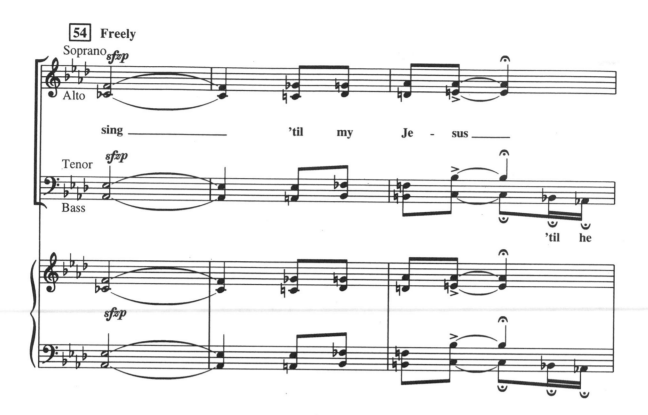

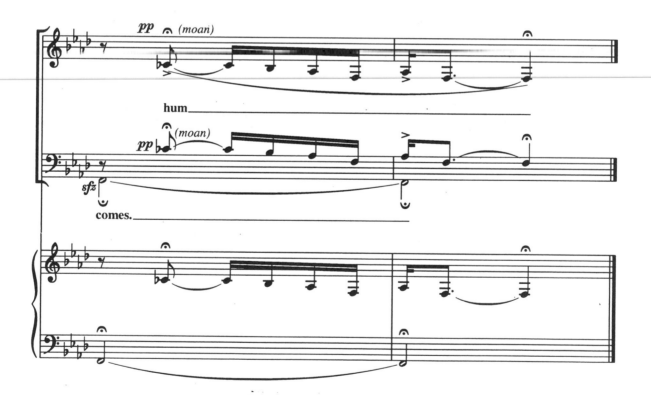

SPOTLIGHT

Careers In Music

Performance

Many people across the United States and around the world make their living through professions associated with music. Some are teachers, composers, conductors, managers, salespersons, technicians and more. One of the more visible careers in music is that of a professional performer. Here a few career opportunities in this area:

Solo Performer

There are many solo artists who make a career of singing classical music, pop, gospel, country and vocal jazz. To make it to the top in a performance career, one must be very talented, as well as someone who is willing to work very hard. It is an extremely competitive field.

To reach this level, you must become proficient in music literacy, have good vocal instruction, develop a large repertoire of songs, have an understanding of contracts and unions, take every opportunity to perform, and develop a reputation for being reliable. Although few soloists reach the top, many maintain a career by doing a variety of jobs.

Professional Choruses

Although not many professional choruses exist in the United States today, there are many symphony and civic groups that use profession singers. Most of these positions are not considered full-time employment. Singing in a civic chorus is an avocation for many.

Broadway and Opera

Many professional singers pursue a career in musical theater or opera. These require professional music training. One must go through a series of auditions to get considered for such a post. If you enjoy acting and singing, then a music theater career may be for you.

If Music Be The Food Of Love

Composer: David C. Dickau
Text: Henry Heveningham
Voicing: SATB

VOCABULARY

- second
- third
- legato
- romantic style

Focus

- Sing music representing the Contemporary period.
- Perform with expressive phrasing.
- Sing close harmony with intervals of a second and third.

Getting Started

"If music be the food of love …"

Any devotee of William Shakespeare can identify these words as the first speech in *Twelfth Night* spoken by Duke Orsino as he calls for music to feed his hunger for love. Orsino continues, "if music be the food of love, play on." But the text of this song is "if music be the food of love, sing on." Has another author boldly altered the bard's famous words?

MUSIC & HISTORY

To learn more about the Contemporary period, see page 140.

◆ History and Culture

Actually, the text of "If Music Be The Food Of Love" is by a relatively obscure sixteenth-century English poet, Colonel Henry Heveningham. His poem shares only the first seven words with Shakespeare. Here is some of each for you to read and compare.

Heveningham:
If music be the food of love
sing on till I am filled with joy;
for then my list'ning soul you move
with pleasures that can never cloy,
your eyes, your mien, your tongue
   declare
that you are music ev'rywhere.

Shakespeare:
If music be the food of love, play on;
Give me excess of it, that, surfeiting,
The appetite may sicken, and so die.
That strain again! it had a dying fall:
O! it came o'er my ear like the sweet
   sound
That breathes upon a bank of violets,
Stealing and giving odour!

Although his style of composing would fit either text, David Dickau (b. 1953) chose Heveningham's words for his expressive song. If you observe the tempo and dynamic markings, the text and music will be eloquent.

Links to Learning

◆ Vocal

By writing harmonies with intervals of a **second** (*an interval of two pitches that are two notes apart*) and a **third** (*an interval of two pitches that are three notes apart*), David Dickau has created a warm and intimate musical work. Sing the E♭ major scale in unison with a full, **legato** (*connected and sustained*) tone. Then, sing the scale in canon, first at the third, then at the interval of a second. Work for accurate intonation.

◆ Artistic Expression

Although a contemporary piece, this work is written in a **romantic style** using *flexible tempo and dynamic markings and a full palate of tonal colors in response to the text.* Make a set of flash cards that include the dynamic and tempo markings found in the music. Some examples include *un poco meno mosso,* and *a tempo.* Write the definition of each term on the back of the card. Work with a classmate and quiz each other on the definitions. How can you use the flash cards to help your choir interpret the music?

Evaluation

Demonstrate how well you have learned the skills and concepts featured in the lesson "If Music Be The Food Of Love" by completing the following:

- Choose any pitch as *do* and sing a major scale. With a classmate, sing the scale in a canon at the third and then as a canon at the second using legato articulation. Evaluate your ability to maintain the correct intervals while performing these canons with a connected and sustained tone.

- Sing measures 39–49 a cappella in an SATB quartet. Devise a way to show the correct flash card as that term is performed in the music. Are there motions you can think of that could also express the flash card terms? Sing and demonstrate these as well.

This work was co-commissioned as a special project of the
Minnesota Music Educators Association and the American Choral Directors Association of Minnesota.

for Anne

If Music Be The Food Of Love

For SATB and Piano

Words by HENRY HEVENINGHAM

Music by DAVID C. DICKAU

The Last Words Of David

Composer: Randall Thompson (1899–1984)
Text: 2 Samuel 23:3–4
Voicing: SATB

VOCABULARY

commission

crescendo

diminuendo

intonation

Focus

- Perform dynamic markings accurately and expressively.
- Sing with accurate intonation and uniform vowel sounds.
- Evaluate musical performance.

 **SPOTLIGHT**

To learn more about careers in music, see page 185.

Getting Started

If you were asked to write a song for someone, you would need to ask yourself some important questions. For what occasion is it being written? What text should I use? What type of group will be singing it? When will it first be performed? Composers might seek answers to these and other questions, if they have been asked to write a musical composition for a special occasion.

◆ History and Culture

"The Last Words Of David" is a composition resulting from a **commission,** *a composer being offered and accepting income to create a composition for a specific purpose or setting.* Prior to 1800, most composers earned their living through patronage to a church or royal court. For example, Baroque composer J. S. Bach (1685–1750) was employed by the church to compose music each week for church events. It was during the Romantic period (1820–1900) that commissions became more prevalent, as composers became more self-sufficient and independent. In 1949, twentieth-century American composer Randall Thompson (1899–1984) was commissioned by the Boston Symphony Orchestra to create a composition in honor of its director, Dr. Serge Koussevitsky. On August 12, 1949, the Boston Symphony Orchestra and the Berkshire Music Center Chorus, led by Dr. Koussevitsky, gave the first public performance of "The Last Words Of David." The premiere provided the listeners with Thompson's answers to the important questions he undoubtedly asked himself as he composed this commissioned work.

Links to Learning

◆ **Vocal**

Perform the following example to help develop phrase shaping. Observe the **crescendo** ◁══════, *a dynamic marking that indicates to gradually sing louder,* and **diminuendo** ══════▷ , *a dynamic marking that indicates to gradually sing softer,* to help you shape the phrase.

Read and perform the following example, focusing on shaping and sustaining uniform vowel sounds to help maintain **intonation** *(in-tune singing)* as you perform.

Evaluation

Demonstrate how well you have learned the skills and concepts featured in the lesson "The Last Words Of David" by completing the following:

* Sing expressively from measures 31–39, paying careful attention to the written dynamics. As you perform, show your understanding of dynamic markings by sitting for softer dynamics and standing for louder dynamics. How well did you do?

* Sing measures 15–25 with one singer on a part. Evaluate your ability to perform with accurate intonation and uniform vowel sounds.

To Dr. Serge Koussevitsky

The Last Words Of David

For SATB and Piano

Words from 2 Samuel 23:3-4

Music by RANDALL THOMPSON

Pingos D'água

Composer: Henrique de Curitiba, edited by Eduardo Lakschevitz and Henry Leck
Text: Portuguese Brazilian Proverb
Voicing: SATB

VOCABULARY

word painting

chromatic scale

Contemporary period

mixed meter

Focus

- Perform music representing the Contemporary period.
- Read, write and perform complex rhythmic patterns.
- Create artistic effects using the voice.

Getting Started

Think about all the sounds that water can make. It may be the crashing waves of the ocean, a water fountain on a hot summer day, a gentle rain, or the roar of Niagara Falls. Now imagine water dripping on a flat stone. The sound of water can be soothing or irritating, depending on where it is found and how it is used. Brainstorm some other places where the sounds of water can be heard. In each case, describe the sound of the water. Listen to the words that others choose in their descriptions. Are the sounds primarily associated with gentleness or forcefulness, or some other feeling? "Pingos D'água" means "drops of water" and employs **word painting,** *a technique in which the music reflects the meaning of the words.* This piece brings to life, through music, the sounds of water.

◆ History and Culture

Henrique de Curitiba (b. 1934) is a Brazilian composer who was born in the city of Curitiba, in southern Brazil. He studied composition in the United States, earning a Master of Music degree at Ithaca College in New York. He is well known in Brazil as a composer, and has many works published both in his native country and in Europe. He wrote "Pingos D'água" under the spell of a misty winter evening, while listening to the monotonous falling drops of rain.

SPOTLIGHT

To learn more about the physiology of singing, see page 57.

Links to Learning

◆ Vocal

The **chromatic scale** is *a scale that consists of half steps and uses all twelve pitches in an octave.* Sing the following ascending chromatic scale on solfège syllables to practice tuning altered pitches as found in "Pingos D'água."

do   di   re   ri   mi   fa   fi   sol   si   la   te   ti   do

◆ Theory

This piece is from the **Contemporary period** *(1900–present).* Characteristics of music from this period include the use of complex rhythms, the chromatic scale, or altered pitches, and **mixed meter** *(a technique in which the time signature or meter changes frequently within a piece of music).* Sing the following example on numbers that represent the number of beats per measure. How many times does the meter change?

◆ Artistic Expression

Think of sounds that you can create that could represent water, such as a pop or splashing sound. Make these sounds with your mouth or with body percussion. Using the rhythms in measure 7, create a repeating layered pattern with some of these "water" sounds.

Evaluation

Demonstrate how well you have learned the skills and concepts featured in the lesson "Pingos D'água" by completing the following:

- Perform measures 19–37 in a quartet. Evaluate your ability to read and perform complex rhythmic patterns.

- Create and notate a 16- to 24-measure composition using your own rhythms and water sounds. Use at least three different meters to demonstrate your understanding of mixed meter. Perform your composition for the class with several friends. Evaluate the creativity and artistry of the vocal sounds in your composition.

Pingos D'água

For SATB, a cappella

Edited by EDUARDO LAKSCHEVITZ
and HENRY LECK

Words and Music by
HENRIQUE DE CURITIBA

Sing the syllables of the two words in a percussive way, sustaining the sound of the consonants

*The Sopranos may sing the following three measures (25-27) without text, vocalizing on "ah."

SPOTLIGHT

Improvisation

Improvisation is *the art of singing or playing music, making it up as you go.* **Scat singing** is *an improvisational style of singing that uses nonsense syllables instead of words.* Sometimes these nonsense sounds can imitate the sound of an instrument. Scat singing, especially as a solo, can be the scariest part of singing jazz.

According to Dr. Kirby Shaw, one of the top vocal jazz composers and conductors in the world today, here are some suggestions to help build your confidence in this fun and exciting art form.

- Start your scat solo with a short melodic or rhythmic idea from the tune being performed. There is nothing wrong in having a preconceived idea before starting to sing a scat solo! By gradually developing the idea as you sing, you will have an organized solo that sounds completely improvised.

- Start with scat syllables like "doo" when singing swing tunes. Try "bee," "dee," and "dn" for occasional accented eighth notes on the upbeats of beats (1 *and* 2 *and* 3 *and* 4 *and*). Try "doot" or "dit" for short last notes of a musical phrase.

- Be able to imitate any sound you like from the world around you, such as a soft breeze, a car horn or a musical instrument. There might be a place for that sound in one of your solos.

- Listen to and imitate note-for-note the great jazz singers or instrumentalists. Musicians like Ella Fitzgerald, Jon Hendricks, Louis Armstrong or Charlie Parker can be an inspiration to you.

- Learn to sing the blues. You can listen to artists like B.B. King, Stevie Ray Vaughan, Buddy Guy or Luther Allison. There are many recordings from which to choose.

In short, learn as many different kinds of songs as you can. The best scat singers quote from such diverse sources as nursery rhymes, African chant and even opera. Above all, have fun as you develop your skills!

Composer/arranger Kirby Shaw's music has been sung around the world and has sold millions of copies. As a performer, Dr. Shaw has scatted one-on-one with such notables as Bobby McFerrin, Al Jarreau, Jon Hendricks and Mark Murphy. As a member of the ensemble, he enjoys singing vocal jazz with Just 4 Kicks, a zany four-man a cappella vocal jazz ensemble.

A Rose Touched By The Sun's Warm Rays

Composer: Jean Berger
Text: Maria Brubacher, translation by Jean Berger
Voicing: SATB

VOCABULARY

dissonance

consonance

interval

second

seventh

SKILL BUILDERS

To learn more about intervals, see Advanced Sight-Singing, *pages 23–24.*

Focus

- Recognize and hear dissonant intervals and chord tones.

- Identify intervals of the second and seventh in music.

Getting Started

In every life there will be good times and bad times, harmony and discord. Do you agree that the contrast created between difficulty and ease in your life can make easy times even sweeter? Many people feel this way about music. Some of the most beautiful musical effects occur with simple musical devices, such as **dissonance** *(a combination of pitches or tones that clash)* and **consonance** *(harmonies in chords or music that are pleasing to the ear)*. However, each term is actually incapable of precise definition since what is dissonant and consonant is subjective to the ear and has evolved through the ages. Most people can agree that certain **intervals** *(the distance between two notes)* have a dissonant quality. One of these dissonances is the interval of a **second** *(an interval of two pitches that are two notes apart)*. A second can be created anytime two syllables, such as *do* and *re*, are sung at the same time. Another dissonance is the **seventh** *(an interval of two pitches that are seven notes apart)*.

◆ History and Culture

Jean Berger (1909–2002), although considered an American composer, was born in Hamm, Germany. He was a choral conductor, arranger, accompanist and musicologist who specialized in medieval and early-seventeenth-century music. This work is the third of four devotional songs that use a Pennsylvania Dutch text.

Links to Learning

◆ Theory

The interval of a second can be heard by singing up and down a major scale in a canon. Sing the example below in two groups. When the first group sings *re*, the second group begins on *do*. Do you hear the dissonance of the second? Experiment with different combinations of seconds. *Do* up to *ti* is a seventh. What other sevenths can you create using the C major scale?

do re mi fa sol la ti do ti la sol fa mi re do

Perform the following examples using solfège syllables. As you sing each example again, hold the chord on each beat and listen closely. Do the circled notes represent the interval of a second, seventh, or some other interval?

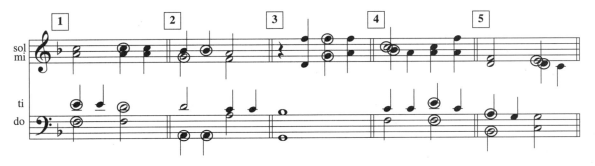

◆ Artistic Expression

Discuss why composers use dissonance. In your opinion, is the use of dissonance effective in this work? What would you change? Why?

Evaluation

Demonstrate how well you have learned the concepts and skills featured in the lesson "A Rose Touched By The Sun's Warm Rays" by completing the following:

- Locate and lightly circle (in pencil) the dissonant intervals in the music. Check your work with a classmate. How well were you able to identify intervals in notation?

- In an SATB quartet, sing the song and raise your hand whenever your part creates dissonance with another part. At least two people should have hands raised on each dissonance. How well are you able to hear dissonance in music being performed?

A Rose Touched By The Sun's Warm Rays

(No. 3 of *Devotional Songs*)

For SATB, a cappella

Words by MARIA BRUBACHER
English Translation by JEAN BERGER

Music by JEAN BERGER

Music with lyrics:

Line 1 (top):
touched by God's great mer - cy, Let joy__ and__ glad - ness
Gna - de dich be - rüh - ret, Lass auch__ dein__ Herz be -

Line 2:
touched by God's great mer - cy, Let joy__ and__ glad - ness, glad - ness
Gna - de dich be - rüh - ret, Lass auch__ dein__ Herz, dein Herz be -

Line 3:
So you, when touched by God's great mer - cy, Let glad - ness and
Wann Got - tes Gna - de dich be - rüh - ret, Lass dein Herz, lass dein

Line 4:
un - - fold; Let joy and glad - ness
und froh; Lass auch dein Herz be -

Second system:

Line 1:
[1] win your soul. A rose touched [2] *molto ritard.* win your soul.___
wir - ken so. Ein Blüm - lein wir - ken so.___

Line 2:
win your soul. A rose touched win, glad-ness win your soul.
wir - ken so. Ein Blüm - lein wir - ken, be - wir - ken so.

Line 3:
joy win__ your soul. A rose, a joy win__ your soul.
Herz be - wir - ken so. Ein Blüm - lein, ein Herz be - wir - ken so.

Line 4:
win your soul. A rose, a win your soul.
wir - ken so. Ein Blüm - lein, ein wir - ken so.___

Set Me As A Seal

Composer: René Clausen
Text: Song of Solomon 8:6–7
Voicing: SATB divsi

VOCABULARY

staggered breathing

diatonic scale

chromatic scale

Focus

- Sing long phrases in a sustained style using staggered breathing.

- Read and perform music employing chromatic alteration.

 **SKILL BUILDERS**

To learn more about the chromatic scale, see Advanced Sight-Singing, *page 9.*

Getting Started

"Set Me As A Seal" is a song about commitment. It is a statement of love and trust. We sometimes hear the words read or sung during weddings. The biblical text from the book of Solomon describes the permanence of love when two people dedicate themselves to one another. The text reads, "Many waters cannot quench love neither can the floods drown it." Love is described as never-ending, and yet never without test or trial. True love will endure despite every test, including death itself. As you learn "Set Me As A Seal," listen for the brilliant manner in which the composer has beautifully expressed the commitment of love through music.

◆ History and Culture

René Clausen is the conductor of The Concordia Choir of Concordia College, Moorhead, Minnesota. Additionally, he is the artistic director of the award-winning Concordia Christmas Concerts, which are frequently featured by PBS stations throughout the nation. His compositional style is varied and eclectic, ranging from works appropriate for high school and church choirs to more technically demanding compositions for college and professional choirs. Clausen was at one time a very gifted golfer. We are fortunate he chose to make his profession in music.

Links to Learning

◆ Vocal

"Set Me As A Seal" requires singing long phrases in a sustained style. If you cannot sing to the end of a phrase without a breath, then use the technique of **staggered breathing** (*the practice of planning breaths so that no two singers take a breath at the same time, thus creating the overall effect of continuous singing*). Perform the following example on a neutral syllable and plan your breaths for staggered breathing.

◆ Theory

A **diatonic scale** is *a scale that uses no altered pitches or accidentals.* "Set Me As A Seal" uses the D major scale for most of the piece. At other times, the composer alters some of the pitches with accidentals. Perform the following descending diatonic scale (example 1) and the descending **chromatic scale** (example 2), *a scale that consists of all half steps and uses all twelve pitches in an octave.*

Evaluation

Demonstrate how well you have learned the skills and concepts featured in the lesson "Set Me As A Seal" by completing the following:

- Perform "Set Me As A Seal" on solfège syllables with eight singers, two per part. Evaluate your ability to sing the correct pitches on the correct syllables, especially the chromatically altered notes.

- In small groups, demonstrate your knowledge of staggered breathing by singing the text expressively to each phrase end with no audible breaths within phrases. When you must quietly breathe, audibly snap your fingers or tap your lap. Notice when others are snapping or tapping their lap. Evaluate your ability to breathe when no one else is taking a breath.

Set Me As A Seal

From *A New Creation*

For SATB divisi, a cappella

Based on Song of Solomon

Music by RENÉ CLAUSEN

seal upon your heart, as a seal up-on your arm, for love is

seal upon your heart, as a seal up-on your seal up-on your arm, love is

seal up-on your heart, as a seal up-on your arm, love is

seal upon your heart, as a seal up-on your arm, love is

strong as death. Ma-ny wa-ters can-not quench love; neither can the floods

strong as death. Ma-ny wa-ters can-not quench love; neither can the floods

strong as death. Ma-ny wa - - ters

strong as death. Ma-ny wa - - ters

seal up-on your heart, as a seal up - on your arm, for

seal up - on your heart, as a seal up - on your, seal up-on your arm,

seal up-on your heart, as a seal up - on your arm,

seal up-on your heart, as a seal up - on your arm,

love is strong as death.

love is strong as death, is strong as death.

love is strong as death, is strong as death.

love is strong as death, is strong as death.

Skylark

Composer: Hoagy Carmichael, arranged by Mac Huff
Text: Johnny Mercer
Voicing: SATB

VOCABULARY

jazz

improvisation

scat singing

Focus

- Sing in a jazz ballad style.
- Improvise using scat singing techniques.

 SPOTLIGHT

To learn more about improvisation and vocal jazz, see pages 215 and 235.

Getting Started

Jazz is *an original American style of music that features swing rhythms, syncopation and improvisation.* The origin of the word *jazz* (originally "jass") is obscure, but the word first appeared in print in 1917 and was associated with social dancing. Early jazz was rarely written down, and some players did not even read music. Players practiced **improvisation** *(the art of singing or playing music, making it up as you go, or composing and performing a melody at the same time)* of new melodies on their instruments or with their voices, thus creating a different performance every time. Vocal improvisations employ **scat singing** *(an improvisational style of singing that uses nonsense syllables instead of words)* to imitate the sounds of jazz instruments.

◆ History and Culture

The great American songwriter Hoagy Carmichael (1899–1981) was greatly influenced by the African American ragtime pianist Reginald DuValle. Carmichael wrote many works that remain popular today. He also composed for Hollywood films and won an Academy Award for the film song "In The Cool, Cool, Cool Of The Evening." His two most popular and enduring songs are "Skylark" and "Stardust." "Skylark" seems to have the element of improvisation built into the work. It has a striking, eloquent, lyrical melody with deep jazz influences that dominate the other musical elements. Hoagy Carmichael earned a bachelor's degree in 1925 and a law degree in 1926 from Indiana University.

Links to Learning

◆ **Vocal**

Vocal improvisation using scat singing requires you to improvise melody notes that fit into the chords of the song, and to make up nonsense syllables with jazz rhythms. Perform the following notated "improvisation" in your own range while the piano plays the accompaniment in measures 7–14. Repeat it a few times. Listen for how the notes fit the piano chords.

◆ **Artistic Expression**

Singing a jazz ballad requires special attention to style and vocal production. The singing should be well supported and free, but with lightness and clarity of tone. Listening to professional jazz recordings is an excellent way to get this sound in your ear.

Evaluation

Demonstrate how well you have learned the skills and concepts featured in the lesson "Skylark" by completing the following:

- With one singer on each part, sing measures 15–22, demonstrating a well-supported, free, light and clear tone. Evaluate your ability to produce the clear, in-tune singing needed to make this song sound appropriate as a jazz ballad.

- Improvise a new scat solo while the piano plays measures 7–14. Allow your ear and musical creativity to lead you to new musical ideas. The more you do it, the better you will get at it! Record yourself scat singing and evaluate how well you are progressing in the art of scat singing.

Skylark

For SATB and Piano

Arranged by
MAC HUFF

Words by JOHNNY MERCER
Music by HOAGY CARMICHAEL

Lyrics:

Sky-lark, _____ have you an-y-thing to say to me? _____ Won't you tell me where my love can be?

Is there a mead-ow in the mist, where some-one's wait-ing to be kissed? ___

15 With a pulse

Sky - lark, have you seen a val - ley green with spring, ___

where my heart can go a - jour - ney-ing, ___ o - ver the shad-ows and the

SPOTLIGHT

Vocal Jazz

Vocal jazz expert Stephen Zegree was asked to share his ideas on vocal jazz. This is what he had to say:

"Vocal jazz is probably the newest and most dynamic trend in choral music education. Traditional classical concert choir literature has been sung for over 500 years, but jazz choir literature has been available to students like you for only the past thirty years. It can be quite challenging to learn, but it almost always is FUN to study and perform.

Why should vocal jazz be an important part of your music education?

- Jazz music was born and raised in the United States. It is our unique musical contribution to the world. It is important to celebrate and embrace the music that comes from our own history and cultural experience.

- The source of much of our vocal jazz repertoire is the songs written by the great American songwriters. Composers such as George Gershwin, Duke Ellington, Richard Rodgers, Irving Berlin, Cole Porter, Jerome Kern and Harold Arlen (and their lyricists) are responsible for the art songs of our country and of the twentieth century.

- Through the study of vocal jazz you have the opportunity to develop your aural skills, creativity and overall musicianship through better understanding of rhythm, harmony and improvisation.

There are many excellent professional vocal groups who have made recordings that I would highly recommend listening to for a better understanding and appreciation for this excellent art form. These groups include The Manhattan Transfer, The Real Group, New York Voices, The Singers Unlimited and Take Six. Some of the greatest solo jazz singers whose recordings and videos you can find include Ella Fitzgerald, Sarah Vaughan, Billie Holiday, Carmen McRae, Mel Torme, Mark Murphy, Bobby McFerrin, Kurt Elling and Nat 'King' Cole.

By all means, make vocal jazz an important part of your musical life."

Stephen Zegree is a professor of music at Western Michigan University, where he teaches piano and jazz, performs with the Western Jazz Quartet, and conducts Gold Company, an internationally recognized jazz-show vocal ensemble. The winner of numerous competitions, awards and honors, Dr. Zegree is in demand as a guest conductor, pianist, clinician and adjudicator around the world.

Somewhere

Composer: Leonard Bernstein (1918–1990), arranged by Robert Edgerton
Text: Stephen Sondheim
Voicing: SATB divisi

VOCABULARY

quarter note triplet

ostinato

Focus

- Sing music representing the Broadway musical.
- Perform rhythm patterns with quarter note triplets.
- Describe and sing an *ostinato*.

Getting Started

Romeo, Romeo! Wherefore art thou Romeo?

This may well be the most famous line written by William Shakespeare. Do you know which characters speak these other notable quotes in *Romeo and Juliet*?

*What's in a name? That which we call a rose
By any other name would smell as sweet;*

*For never was a story of more woe
Than this of Juliet and her Romeo.*

*But, soft! What light through yonder window breaks?
It is the east, and Juliet is the sun.*

 **SPOTLIGHT**

To learn more about musical theater and vocal jazz, see pages 144 and 235.

◆ History and Culture

When the great choreographer and director Jerome Robbins brought composer Leonard Bernstein and playwright Arthur Laurents together in 1949 to write a musical version of "Romeo and Juliet," they agreed to call it *East Side Story*. Romeo would be a Jewish boy, Juliet an Italian Catholic girl, and the Capulets and Montagues would be clashing street gangs on New York City's lower East Side. However, after a six-year delay for busy schedules, the conflict seemed dated. They turned to a more timely subject, the star-crossed love story of a native-born Polish boy with a newly arrived Puerto Rican immigrant girl. The street gangs would move to the city's West Side. Bernstein chose the young Stephen Sondheim to write the lyrics.

Links to Learning

◆ Theory

A **quarter note triplet** is *three equal divisions of a half note.* Practice the following patterns by clapping or tapping the circled notes while counting the numbers out loud in a steady beat.

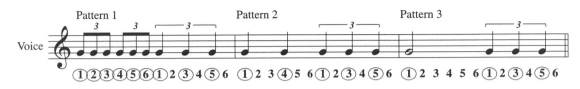

This arrangement of "Somewhere" opens with an **ostinato** (*a rhythmic or melodic passage that is repeated continuously*) in the Bass and Soprano parts. What effect does the ostinato have on the other vocal lines? Can you find any other examples of ostinato used in the music?

◆ Artistic Expression

Read a synopsis of *West Side Story.* List the characters and write a short description for each. Which character sings "Somewhere"? Discuss the plot action before and after the song. How will this information help you interpret the music?

Evaluation

Demonstrate how well you have learned the skills and concepts featured in the lesson "Somewhere" by completing the following:

- With one singer on a part, sing measures 39–43 a cappella. Evaluate your ability to sing the quarter note triplet patterns accurately.

- Write an ostinato for measures 1–11 with new lyrics and rhythm. Perform your ostinato as the class sings. Tape your performance and compare your ostinato to the original one. How are the patterns different? How are they the same? Which ostinato performance do you prefer?

This arrangement dedicated to Simon Carrington, Conductor
North Carolina High School Honors Chorus

Somewhere

From *West Side Story*

For SATB divisi, a cappella

Arranged by
ROBERT EDGERTON

Lyrics by STEPHEN SONDHEIM
Music by LEONARD BERNSTEIN

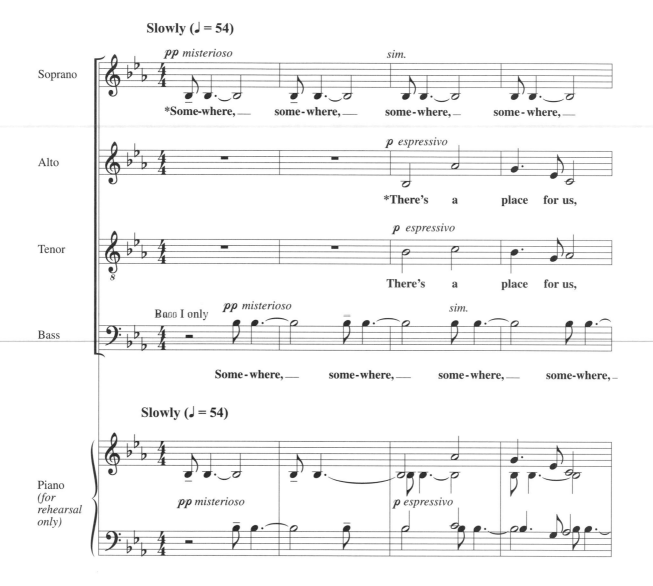

*Divide Soprano II evenly between Soprano and Alto measures 1–11 and 31–38.

238 **Advanced Mixed**

some-where, — some-where, — some-where, — some-where, —

poco cresc. 3

Some-where a place for us. Peace and qui-et and o - pen air

poco cresc. 3

Some-where a place for us. Peace and qui-et and o - pen air

some-where, — some-where, — some-where, — some-where, —

poco cresc. 3

5

poco dim. A *p warmly*

some-where, — some-where, — some - where. There's a

poco dim. *p warmly*

wait for us some-where. ——— There's a

poco dim. *p warmly*

wait for us some-where. ——— There's a

poco dim. All Basses *p warmly*

some-where, — some - where, some - where. There's a

A

poco dim. *p warmly*

9

SPOTLIGHT

Vocal Health

Since our voices are a result of physical processes in our bodies, we need to learn a few things we can do to ensure that our voices will be healthy and function well for years to come.

To experience, explore and establish good habits for vocal health, try the following:

- Limit shouting and trying to talk over loud noise.
- Do not smoke. Avoid smoky environments.
- Avoid beverages with caffeine and fried foods (acid reflux).
- Limit talking on the telephone. Use a supported voice when you do.
- Avoid whispering if you lose your voice.
- Rest your voice if it is tired or if it takes more muscular effort to sing.
- Keep your voice hydrated. Drink lots of water every day and use nonmentholated, sugar-free lozenges if your throat is dry.
- Gargle with warm salt water if your throat is sore.
- Use a humidifier in your bedroom when the air conditioning or furnace is on.
- Try not to clear your throat. Swallow or clear with a puff of air instead.
- Avoid coughing, if at all possible.
- Cover your nose and mouth with a scarf in cold weather.
- Get plenty of sleep, especially the night before a performance.

As you can see, maintaining good vocal health is a matter of common sense in taking care of your body. By taking good care of yourself, you can continue to enjoy a strong, healthy singing voice. Take care and sing long!

Sorida

Composer: Rosephanye Powell
Text: Rosephanye Powell
Voicing: SATB divisi

VOCABULARY

syncopation

triplet

interlocking

Focus

- Perform music with syncopation and triplets.
- Create and demonstrate layered texture in music and art.
- Sing music representing the African culture.

Getting Started

Can you think of anything that would connect the Sears Tower in Chicago, Illinois, with the following?

a. a wedding cake

b. the Grand Canyon in Arizona

c. the *Canon in D* by Johann Pachelbel

d. a song from Zimbabwe

The connection lies in the structure of "Sorida." Take a minute to look through the music and you will see that it is constructed of layers of interlocking percussion and voice stacked on top of each other, building in texture, density and volume. That's the relationship with the items on the list. In each instance, adding layers to a solid foundation has created something complex and wonderful.

SPOTLIGHT

To learn more about vocal health, see page 245.

◆ History and Culture

Although not a traditional song, "Sorida" shares the joy and spontaneity found in much of the folk music of Zimbabwe. Approximately the size of Montana, Zimbabwe is a landlocked country in South Africa. The Shona people constitute the majority of the population. "Sorida" is a Shona word of greeting.

"Sorida" should be performed in a jubilant manner, engaging your whole being. Body movement, especially swaying, is encouraged. Think about different ways to begin the song. You could begin with a sustained drum roll, or a series of percussive patterns that can be added one at a time. In any case, as you learn each vocal layer of the musical texture, let the music build with energy and life!

Links to Learning

◆ **Theory**

The use of **syncopation,** *the placement of accents on a weak beat, or a weak portion of the beat,* and **triplets,** *a group of notes in which three notes of equal duration are sung in the time normally given to two notes of equal duration,* add rhythmic energy to "Sorida." Clap or tap the following patterns for rhythmic accuracy. Perform all four patterns, without stopping, in different orders such as ACDB, DACB, ADBC, and so forth. Perform the example as a rhythmic round with several other people and listen for the **interlocking** *(short melodic or rhythmic patterns performed simultaneously that fit together to create a continuous musical texture)* of the parts.

◆ **Artistic Expression**

Research traditional Zimbabwe shapes and designs. Start a sketch for a "Sorida" wall hanging that will use layers of design to represent each percussion and voice part. How can your design help you interpret each phrase? Here are a few traditional designs to get you started:

Evaluation

Demonstrate how well you have learned the skills and concepts featured in the lesson "Sorida" by completing the following:

- With one singer on each part, sing measures 7–30. Evaluate how well you were able to sing the syncopation and triplet rhythms with clarity and accuracy.

- Using the colors of the Zimbabwe flag (green, yellow, red, black and white) create a layered design that represents measures 58–66. Choose shapes and sizes to reflect the contour and style of each musical line. Use the ideas in your design to interpret the music as you perform.

For Dr. André J. Thomas, Director of Choral Activities, Florida State University

Sorida
(A Zimbabwe Greeting)

For SATB divisi with Optional African Percussion

Words and Music by
ROSEPHANYE POWELL

*Duet optional, higher notes can be omitted when sung as a solo.
**Optional sacred text

*Trio optional, middle notes should be sung as solo.

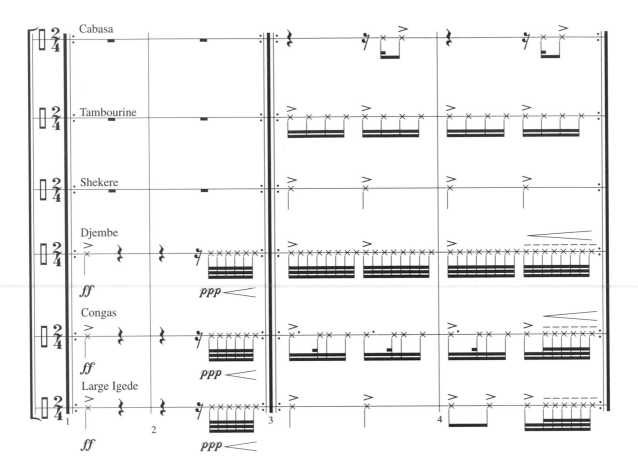

Performance Notes

Sorida should be performed in a jubilant manner. The singers and percussionists should engage their whole being when performing this song. Body movement is encouraged, especially swaying. There are numerous ways to begin the song. It may begin with the percussion patterns of measures 1-2, or it can begin with all percussion sustaining a roll. Also, the percussion could begin by sustaining a roll while the drums play the patterns of measures 3-4. Generally, once the patterns of measures 3-4 begin (at the beginning or at the entrance of the altos), they should be played throughout the song. However, measures 3-4 can be improvised for variety as long as the percussionists stay within the framework of the original patterns. When the choir sings the final "sorida, sorida," the percussionists should cease playing the patterns and play the rhythm that the choir sings to add a sense of finality.

Glossary

CHORAL MUSIC TERMS

2/2 meter A time signature in which there are two beats per measure and the half note receives the beat.

2/4 meter A time signature in which there are two beats per measure and the quarter note receives the beat.

3/2 meter A time signature in which there are three beats per measure and the half note receives the beat.

3/4 meter A time signature in which there are three beats per measure and the quarter note receives the beat.

3/8 meter A time signature in which there is one group of three eighth notes per measure and the dotted quarter note receives the beat. When the tempo is very slow, this meter can be counted as having three beats per measure, with the eighth note receiving the beat.

4/4 meter A time signature in which there are four beats per measure and the quarter note receives the beat.

5/8 meter A time signature in which there are five beats per measure and the eighth note receives the beat.

6/4 meter A time signature in which there are two groups of three quarter notes per measure and the dotted half note receives the beat. When the tempo is very slow, this meter can be counted as having six beats per measure, with the quarter note receiving the beat.

6/8 meter A time signature in which there are two groups of three eighth notes per measure and the dotted quarter note receives the beat. When the tempo is very slow, this meter can be counted as having six beats per measure, with the eighth note receiving the beat.

9/8 meter A time signature in which there are three groups of three eighth notes per measure and the dotted quarter note receives the beat. When the tempo is very slow, this meter can be counted as having nine beats per measure, with the eighth note receiving the beat.

12/8 meter A time signature in which there are four groups of three eighth notes per measure and the dotted quarter note receives the beat.

A

a cappella *(ah-kah-PEH-lah)* [It.] A style of singing without instrumental accompaniment.

a tempo *(ah TEM-poh)* [It.] A tempo marking that indicates to return to the original tempo of a piece or section of music.

ABA form A form in which an opening section (A) is followed by a contrasting section (B), which leads to the repetition of the opening section (A).

accelerando *(accel.) (ah-chel-leh-RAHN-doh)* [It.] A tempo marking that indicates to gradually get faster.

accent A symbol placed above or below a given note to indicate that the note should receive extra emphasis or stress. (>)

accidental Any sharp, flat or natural that is not included in the key signature of a piece of music.

adagio *(ah-DAH-jee-oh)* [It.] Slow tempo, but not as slow as *largo*.

ad libitum *(ad. lib.)* [Lt.] An indication that the performer may vary the tempo or add or delete a vocal or instrumental part.

Aeolian scale *(ay-OH-lee-an)* [Gk.] A modal scale that starts and ends on *la*. It is made up of the same arrangement of whole and half steps as a natural minor scale.

al fine *(ahl FEE-neh)* [It.] To the end.

aleatory music *(AY-lee-uh-toh-ree)* A type of music in which certain aspects are performed randomly. Also known as *chance music*.

alla breve Indicates cut time; a duple meter in which there are two beats per measure, and the half note receives the beat. *See* cut time.

allargando (*allarg.*) (*ahl-ahr-GAHN-doh*) [It.] To broaden, become slower.

allegro (*ah-LEH-groh*) [It.] Brisk tempo; faster than *moderato*, slower than *vivace*.

allegro non troppo (*ah-LEH-groh nohn TROH-poh*) [It.] A tempo marking that indicates "not too fast." Not as fast as *allegro*.

altered pitch Another name for an accidental.

alto (*AL-toh*) The lowest-sounding female voice.

andante (*ahn-DAHN-teh*) [It.] Moderately slow; a walking tempo.

andante con moto (*ahn-DAHN-teh kohn MOH-toh*) [It.] A slightly faster tempo, "with motion."

andantino (*ahn-dahn-TEE-noh*) [It.] A tempo marking that means "little walking," a little faster than *andante*.

animato Quickly, lively; "animated."

anthem A choral composition in English using a sacred text.

answer In a fugue, the entry of the theme at a different pitch, usually the interval of a fourth or fifth away, than that of the original subject.

antiphon In the Roman Catholic liturgy, a chant with a prose text connected with the psalm, sung by two choirs in alternation. The *antiphon* is usually a refrain for the psalm or canticle verses. Its melodies are often simple, with only one note per syllable.

arpeggio (*ahr-PEH-jee-oh*) [It.] A chord in which the pitches are sounded successively, usually from lowest to highest; in broken style.

arrangement A piece of music in which a composer takes an existing melody and adds extra features or changes the melody in some way.

arranger A composer who takes an original or existing melody and adds extra features or changes the melody in some way.

art songs Musical settings of poetry. Songs about life, love and human relationships that are written by a professional composer and have a serious artistic purpose, as opposed to a popular song or folk song.

articulation The amount of separation or connection between notes.

articulators The lips, teeth, tongue and other parts of the mouth and throat that are used to produce vocal sound.

avant-garde A term used in the arts to denote those who make a radical departure from tradition.

avocational Not related to a job or career.

B

ballad A strophic folk song with a distinctly narrative element. Ballads tell stories.

barbershop A style of *a cappella* singing in which three parts harmonize with the melody. The lead sings the melody while the tenor harmonizes above and the baritone and bass harmonize below.

barcarole A Venetian boat song.

baritone The male voice between tenor and bass.

barline A vertical line placed on the musical staff that groups notes and rests together.

Baroque period (*bah-ROHK*) [Fr.] The historical period in Western civilization from 1600 to 1750.

bass The lowest-sounding male voice.

bass clef A clef that generally indicates notes that sound lower than middle C.

basso continuo (*BAH-soh cun-TIN-you-oh*) [It.] A continually moving bass line, common in music from the Baroque period.

beat The steady pulse of music.

bebop style Popular in jazz, music that features notes that are light, lively and played quickly. Often, the melodic lines are complex and follow unpredictable patterns.

blues scale An altered major scale that uses flatted or lowered third, fifth and seventh notes: *ma* (lowered from *mi*), *se* (lowered from *sol*) and *te* (lowered from *ti*).

blues style An original African American art form that developed in the early twentieth century in the Mississippi Delta region of the South. The lyrics often express feelings of frustration, hardship or longing. It often contains elements such as call and response, the blues scale and swing.

breath mark A symbol in vocal music used to indicate where a singer should take a breath. (')

breath support A constant airflow necessary to produce sound for singing.

C

cadence A melodic or harmonic structure that marks the end of a phrase or the completion of a song.

call and response A derivative of the field hollers used by slaves as they worked. A leader or group sings a phrase (call) followed by a response of the same phrase by another group.

calypso A style of music that originated in the West Indies and which features syncopated rhythms and comical lyrics.

canon A musical form in which one part sings a melody, and the other parts sing the same melody, but enter at different times. Canons are sometimes called *rounds*.

cantabile *(con-TAH-bee-leh)* [It.] In a lyrical, singing style.

cantata *(con-TAH-tah)* [It.] A large-scale musical piece made up of several movements for singers and instrumentalists. Johann Sebastian Bach was a prominent composer of cantatas.

cantor *(CAN-tor)* A person who sings and/or teaches music in a temple or synagogue.

canzona [It.] A rhythmic instrumental composition that is light and fast-moving.

carol A strophic song of the Middle Ages, sung in English or Latin, beginning with a refrain that is then repeated after each verse. In recent times, the word *carol* refers to a strophic song about Christmas or the Virgin Mary.

chamber music Music performed by a small instrumental ensemble, generally with one instrument per part. The string quartet is a popular form of chamber music, consisting of two violins, a viola and a cello. Chamber music was popular during the Classical period.

chanson *(shaw[n]-SOH[N])* [Fr.] Literally "song" in French, a *chanson* is a vocal composition to French words. The rich history of the *chanson* dates back to the late Middle Ages and continues to the present day, incorporating many styles and composers.

chantey *See* sea chantey.

chanteyman A soloist who improvised and led the singing of sea chanteys.

chest voice The lower part of the singer's vocal range.

chorale *(kuh-RAL)* [Gr.] Congregational song or hymn of the German Protestant Church.

chord The combination of three or more notes played or sung together at the same time.

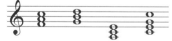

chromatic Moving by half-steps. Also, notes foreign to a scale.

chromatic scale *(kroh-MAT-tick)* [Gk.] A scale that consists of all half steps and uses all twelve pitches in an octave.

Classical period The historical period in Western civilization from 1750 to 1820.

clef   The symbol at the beginning of a staff that indicates which lines and spaces represent which notes.

close harmony   Harmony in which notes of the chord are kept as close together as possible, often within an octave.

coda   A special ending to a song. A concluding section of a composition. (𝄌)

Collegium musicum (*col-LAY-gee-oom MOO-zee-koom*) [Lat.] A musical group, usually at a university, that presents period-style performances of Renaissance and Baroque music.

commission   A musical work created by the composer for a specific event or purpose. The composer is approached by the commissioning organization (orchestra, chorus, academic institution, church) or individual, and an acceptable fee is agreed upon.

common time   Another name for 4/4 meter. Also known as common meter. (𝄴)

composer   A person who takes a musical thought and writes it out in musical notation to share it with others.

compound meter   Any meter in which the dotted quarter note receives the beat, and the division of the beat is based on three eighth notes. 6/8, 9/8 and 12/8 are examples of compound meter.

con moto (*kohn MOH-toh*) [It.] With motion.

concert etiquette   A term used to describe what is appropriate behavior in formal or informal musical performances.

concerto (*cun-CHAIR-toh*) [Fr., It.] A composition for a solo instrument and orchestra.

concerto grosso (*cun-CHAIR-toh GROH-soh*) [Fr., It.] A multimovement Baroque piece for a group of soloists and an orchestra.

conductor   A person who uses hand and arm gestures to interpret the expressive elements of music for singers and instrumentalists.

conductus   A thirteenth-century song for two, three or four voices.

consonance   Harmonies in chords or music that are pleasing to the ear.

Contemporary period   The historical period from 1900 to the present.

countermelody   A separate melodic line that supports and/or contrasts the melody of a piece of music.

counterpoint   The combination of two or more melodic lines. The parts move independently while harmony is created. Johann Sebastian Bach is considered by many to be one of the greatest composers of contrapuntal music.

contrary motion   A technique in which two melodic lines move in opposite directions.

crescendo (*creh-SHEN-doh*) [It.] A dynamic marking that indicates to gradually sing or play louder. ◁▬

cumulative song   A song form in which more words are added each time a verse is sung.

cut time   Another name for 2/2 *meter*. (𝄵)

D

da capo (*D.C.*) (*dah KAH-poh*) [It.] Go back to the beginning and repeat; *see also* dal segno *and* al fine.

dal segno (*D.S.*) (*dahl SAYN-yah*) [It.] Go back to the sign and repeat.

D. C. al Fine (*FEE-nay*) [It.] A term that indicates to go back to the beginning and repeat. The term *al fine* indicates to sing to the end, or *fine*.

decrescendo (*DAY-creh-shen-doh*) [It.] A dynamic marking that indicates to gradually sing or play softer. ▷▬

descant   A special part in a piece of music that is usually sung higher than the melody or other parts of the song.

diatonic interval   The distance between two notes that are indigenous to a major or minor scale.

diatonic scale (*die-uh-TAH-nick*) A scale that uses no altered pitches or accidentals. Both the major scale and the natural minor scale are examples of a diatonic scale.

diction   The pronunciation of words while singing.

diminished chord   A minor chord in which the top note is lowered one half step from *mi* to *me*.

diminuendo (*dim.*) (*duh-min-yoo-WEN-doh*) [It.] Gradually getting softer; *see also* decrescendo.

diphthong   A combination of two vowel sounds.

dissonance   A combination of pitches or tones that clash.

dolce (*DOHL-chay*)   [It.] Sweetly.

dominant chord   A chord built on the fifth note of a scale. In a major scale, this chord uses the notes *sol, ti* and *re*, and it may be called the **V** ("five") chord. In a minor scale, this chord uses the notes *mi, sol* and *ti* (or *mi, si* and *ti*), and it may be called the **v** or **V** ("five") chord.

Dorian scale (*DOOR-ee-an*)   [Gk.] A modal scale that starts and ends on *re*.

dot   A symbol that increases the length of a given note by half its value. It is placed to the right of the note.

dotted half note   A note that represents three beats of sound when the quarter note receives the beat. ♩.

dotted rhythms   A dot after a note lengthens the note by one-half its original value. When notes are paired, the first note is often three times longer than the note that follows (e.g., dotted half note followed by quarter note, dotted quarter note followed by eighth note, dotted eighth note followed by sixteenth note).

double barline   A set of two barlines that indicate the end of a piece or section of music.

D. S. al coda (*dahl SAYN-yoh ahl KOH-dah*) [It.] Repeat from the symbol (𝄋) and skip to the coda when you see the sign. (⊕)

duet   A group of two singers or instrumentalists.

duple   Notes in equal groups of two.

dynamics   Symbols in music that indicate how loud or soft to sing or play.

E

eighth note   A note that represents one-half beat of sound when the quarter note receives the beat. Two eighth notes equal one beat of sound when the quarter note receives the beat.

eighth rest   A rest that represents one-half beat of silence when the quarter note receives the beat. Two eighth rests equal one beat of silence when the quarter note receives the beat.

expressionism   Music of the early twentieth century, usually associated with Germany, that was written in a deeply subjective and introspective style.

expressive singing   To sing with feeling.

F

fanfare   A brief celebratory piece, usually performed by brass instruments and percussion, at the beginning of an event.

falsetto   [It.] The register in the male voice that extends far above the natural voice. The light upper range.

fermata (*fur-MAH-tah*)   [It.] A symbol that indicates to hold a note or rest for longer than its given value. (⌢)

fine (*fee-NAY*)   [It.] A term used to indicate the end of a piece of music.

fixed do (*doh*)   A system of syllables in which the note C is always *do*. *See also* movable do.

flat   A symbol that lowers the pitch of a given note by one half step. (♭)

folk music   Music that is passed down from generation to generation through oral tradition. Traditional music that reflects a place, event or a national feeling.

folk song   A song passed down from generation to generation through oral tradition. A song that reflects a place, event or a national feeling.

form   The structure or design of a musical composition.

forte *(FOR-tay)* [It.] A dynamic that indicates to sing or play loud. (*f*)

fortissimo *(for-TEE-see-moh)* [It.] A dynamic that indicates to sing or play very loud. (*ff*)

fugue *(FYOOG)* A musical form in which the same melody is performed by different instruments or voices entering at different times, thus adding layers of sound.

fusion Music that is developed by the act of combining various types and cultural influences of music into a new style.

G

glee A homophonic, unaccompanied English song, usually in three or four vocal parts. The texts of early glees, from the seventeenth century, were usually about eating and drinking, but also about patriotism, hunting and love.

glissando *(glees-SAHN-doh)* An effect produced by sliding from one note to another. The pseudo-Italian word comes from the French word *glisser*, "to slide."

gospel music Religious music that originated in the African American churches of the South. This music can be characterized by improvisation, syncopation and repetition.

gradual In the Roman Catholic liturgy, a chant that follows the reading of the Epistle. The texts are usually from the Psalms. The melodies often contain several notes per syllable. The term *gradual* (from the Latin *gradus*, "a step") is so called because it was sung while the deacon was ascending the steps to sing the Gospel.

grand opera A large-scale opera that is sung throughout, with no spoken dialogue. *See* Singspiel.

grand staff A staff that is created when two staves are joined together.

grandioso [It.] Stately, majestic.

grave *(GRAH-veh)* [It.] Slow, solemn.

grazioso *(grah-tsee-OH-soh)* [It.] Graceful.

Gregorian chant A single, unaccompanied melodic line sung by male voices. Featuring a sacred text and used in the church, this style of music was developed in the medieval period.

guiro *(GWEE-roh)* A Latin American percussion instrument made from an elongated gourd, with notches cut into it, over which a stick is scraped to produce a rasping sound.

H

half note A note that represents two beats of sound when the quarter note receives the beat.

half rest A rest that represents two beats of silence when the quarter note receives the beat.

half step The smallest distance (interval) between two notes on a keyboard; the chromatic scale is composed entirely of half steps.

harmonic intervals Two or more notes that are sung or played simultaneously.

harmonic minor scale A minor scale that uses a raised seventh note, *si* (raised from *sol*).

harmonics Small whistle-like tones, or overtones, that are sometimes produced over a sustained pitch.

harmony A musical sound that is formed when two or more different pitches are played or sung at the same time.

head voice The higher part of the singer's vocal range.

hemiola In early music theory, *hemiola* denotes the ratio 3:2. In the modern metrical system, it refers to the articulation of two bars in triple meter as if they were three bars in duple meter.

High Renaissance The latter part of the Renaissance period, c. 1430–1600.

homophonic *(hah-muh-FAH-nik)* [Gk.] A texture where all parts sing similar rhythm in unison or harmony.

homophony *(haw-MAW-faw-nee)* [Gk.] A type of music in which there are two or more parts with similar or identical rhythms being sung or played at the same time. Also, music in which melodic interest is concentrated in one voice part and may have subordinate accompaniment.

hymn A song or poem that offers praise to God.

I

imitation The act of one part copying what another part has already played or sung.

improvisation The art of singing or playing music, making it up as you go, or composing and performing a melody at the same time.

interlocking Short melodic or rhythmic patterns performed simultaneously that fit together to create a continuous musical texture.

interlude A short piece of music that is used to bridge the acts of a play or the verses of a song or hymn.

International Phonetic Alphabet (IPA) A phonetic alphabet that provides a notational standard for all languages. Developed in Paris, France, in 1886.

interval The distance between two notes.

intonation The accuracy of pitch, in-tune singing.

Ionian scale *(eye-OWN-ee-an)* [Gk.] A modal scale that starts and ends on *do*. It is made up of the same arrangement of whole and half steps as a major scale.

J

jazz An original American style of music that features swing rhythms, syncopation and improvisation.

K

key Determined by a song's or scale's home tone, or keynote.

key signature A symbol or set of symbols that determines the key of a piece of music.

L

Ländler *(LEND-ler)* [Ger.] A slow Austrian dance, performed in 3/4 meter, similar to a waltz.

largo [It.] A tempo marking that indicates a broad, slow, dignified style.

ledger lines Short lines that appear above, between treble and bass clefs, or below the bass clef, used to expand the notation.

legato *(leh-GAH-toh)* [It.] A connected and sustained style of singing and playing.

lento *(LEN-toh)* [It.] Slow; a little faster than *largo*, a little slower than *adagio*.

lied *(leet)* [Ger.] A song in the German language, generally with a secular text.

lieder *(LEE-der)* [Ger.] Plural of *lied*. Songs in the German language, especially art songs of the Romantic period. These songs usually have a secular text.

liturgical text A text that has been written for the purpose of worship in a church setting.

lute An early form of the guitar.

Lydian scale *(LIH-dee-an)* [Gk.] A modal scale that starts and ends on *fa*.

lyricist The writer of the words (lyrics) to a song.

lyrics The words of a song.

M

madrigal A poem that has been set to music in the language of the composer. Featuring several imitative parts, it usually has a secular text and is generally sung *a cappella*.

maestoso (*mah-eh-STOH-soh*) [It.] Perform majestically.

major chord A chord that can be based on the *do, mi,* and *sol* of a major scale.

major scale A scale that has *do* as its home tone, or keynote. It is made up of a specific arrangement of whole steps and half steps in the following order: W + W + H + W + W + W + H.

major second Two notes a whole step apart.

major tonality A song that is based on a major scale with *do* as its keynote, or home tone.

manniboula A rustic pizzicato bass instrument consisting of a wooden resonance box with a rose window on its front panel, where there are three metallic blades that sound when manipulated by the fingers of the player sitting on it. Also called a *manniba.*

marcato (*mar-CAH-toh*) [It.] A stressed and accented style of singing and playing.

Mass A religious service of prayers and ceremonies originating in the Roman Catholic Church consisting of spoken and sung sections. It consists of several sections divided into two groups: proper (text changes for every day) and ordinary (text stays the same in every Mass). Between the years 1400 and 1600, the Mass assumed its present form consisting of the Kyrie, Gloria, Credo, Sanctus and Agnus Dei. It may include chants, hymns and Psalms as well. The Mass also developed into large musical works for chorus, soloists and even orchestra.

measure The space between two barlines.

medieval period The historical period in Western civilization also known as the Middle Ages (400–1430).

medley A collection of songs musically linked together.

melisma (*muh-LIZ-mah*) [Gk.] A group of notes sung to a single syllable or word.

melismatic singing (*muh-liz-MAT-ik*) [Gk.] A style of text setting in which one syllable is sung over many notes.

melodic contour The overall shape of the melody.

melodic minor scale A minor scale that uses raised sixth and seventh notes: *fi* (raised from *fa*) and *si* (raised from *sol*). Often, these notes are raised in ascending patterns, but not in descending patterns.

melody A logical succession of musical tones.

meno mosso (*MEH-noh MOHS-soh*) [It.] A tempo marking that indicates "less motion," or slower.

merengue (*meh-REN-geh*) [Sp.] A Latin American ballroom dance in moderate duple meter with the basic rhythm pattern:

It is the national dance of the Dominican Republic.

messa di voce (*MES-sah dee VOH-cheh*) [It.] A technique of singing a crescendo and decrescendo on a held note. The term literally means "placing of the voice."

meter A way of organizing rhythm.

meter signature *See* time signature.

metronome marking A sign that appears over the top line of the staff at the beginning of a piece or section of music that indicates the tempo. It shows the kind of note that will receive the beat and the number of beats per minute as measured by a metronome.

mezzo forte (*MEH-tsoh FOR tay*) [It.] A dynamic that indicates to sing or play medium loud. (*mf*)

mezzo piano (*MEH-tsoh pee-AH-noh*) [It.] A dynamic that indicates to sing or play medium soft. (*mp*)

mezzo voce (*MEH-tsoh VOH-cheh*) [It.] With half voice; reduced volume and tone.

minor chord A chord that can be based on the *la, do,* and *mi* of a minor scale.

minor scale   A scale that has *la* as its home tone, or keynote. It is made up of a specific arrangement of whole steps and half steps in the following order: W + H +W + W + H + W + W.

minor tonality   A song that is based on a minor scale with *la* as its keynote, or home tone.

minstrel   The term *minstrel* originally referred to a wandering musician from the Middle Ages. In the late nineteenth century, the word was applied to black-face entertainers who presented a variety show consisting of comic songs, sentimental ballads, soft-shoe dancing, clogging, instrumental playing, comedy skits, sight gags and jokes.

missa brevis (*MEES-sah BREH-vees*) [Lat.] Literally, a "brief mass." The term refers to a short setting of the Mass Ordinary.

mixed meter   A technique in which the time signature or meter changes frequently within a piece of music.

Mixolydian scale (*mix-oh-LIH-dee-an*) [Gr.] A modal scale that starts and ends on *sol*.

modal scale   A scale based on a mode. Like major and minor scales, each modal scale is made up of a specific arrangement of whole steps and half steps, with the half steps occurring between *mi* and *fa*, and *ti* and *do*.

mode   An early system of pitch organization that was used before major and minor scales and keys were developed.

modulation   A change in the key or tonal center of a piece of music within the same song.

molto [It.] Very or much; for example, *molto rit.* means "much slower."

monophony (*mon-AH-foh-nee*)   Music with only a single melody line (e.g., Gregorian chant).

motet (*moh-teht*)   Originating as a medieval and Renaissance polyphonic song, this choral form of composition became an unaccompanied work, often in contrapuntal style. Also, a short, sacred choral piece with a Latin text that is used in religious services but is not a part of the regular Mass.

motive   A shortened expression, sometimes contained within a phrase.

moveable do (*doh*)   A system of syllables in which the first note of each diatonic scale is *do*. *See also* fixed do.

music critic   A writer who gives an evaluation of a musical performance.

music notation   Any means of writing down music, including the use of notes, rests and symbols.

musical   A play or film whose action and dialogue are combined with singing and dancing.

musical theater   An art form that combines acting, singing, and dancing to tell a story. It often includes staging, costumes, lighting and scenery.

mysterioso [It.] Perform in a mysterious or haunting way, to create a haunting mood.

N

narrative song   A song that tells a story.

national anthem   A patriotic song adopted by nations through tradition or decree.

nationalism   Patriotism; pride of country. This feeling influenced many Romantic composers such as Wagner, Tchaikovsky, Dvořák, Chopin and Brahms.

natural   A symbol that cancels a previous sharp or flat, or a sharp or flat in a key signature. (♮)

natural minor scale   A minor scale that uses no altered pitches or accidentals.

neoclassicism   Music of the early twentieth century characterized by the inclusion of contemporary styles or features derived from the music of the seventeenth and eighteenth centuries.

New Romanticism A genuine tonal melody composed with exotic textures and timbres.

no breath mark A direction not to take a breath at a specific place in the composition. (N.B.)

non troppo *(nahn TROH-poh)* [It.] Not too much; for example, *allegro non troppo,* "not too fast."

notation Written notes, symbols and directions used to represent music within a composition.

nuance Subtle variations in tempo, phrasing, articulation, dynamics and intonation that are used to enhance a musical performance.

O

octave An interval of two pitches that are eight notes apart on a staff.

ode A poem written in honor of a special person or occasion. These poems were generally dedicated to a member of a royal family. In music, an ode usually includes several sections for choir, soloists and orchestra.

opera A combination of singing, instrumental music, dancing and drama that tells a story.

operetta *(oh-peh-RET-tah)* [It.] A light opera, often with spoken dialogue and dancing.

optional divisi *(opt.div.)* Indicating a split in the music into optional harmony, shown by a smaller cued note.

oral tradition Music that is learned through rote or by ear and is interpreted by its performer(s).

oratorio *(or-uh-TOR-ee-oh)* [It.] A dramatic work for solo voices, chorus and orchestra presented without theatrical action. Usually, oratorios are based on a literary or religious theme.

ostinato *(ahs-tuh-NAH-toh)* [It.] A rhythmic or melodic passage that is repeated continuously.

overture A piece for orchestra that serves as an introduction to an opera or other dramatic work.

P

palate The roof of the mouth; the hard palate is at the front, and the soft palate is at the back.

pambiche *(pahm-BEE-cheh)* [Sp.] A dance that is a slower version of the merengue.

parallel keys Major and minor keys having the same keynote, or home tone (tonic).

parallel minor scale A minor scale that shares the same starting pitch as its corresponding major scale.

parallel motion A technique in which two or more melodic lines move in the same direction.

parallel sixths A group of intervals that are a sixth apart and which move at the same time and in the same direction.

parallel thirds A group of intervals that are a third apart and which move at the same time and in the same direction.

part-singing Two or more parts singing an independent melodic line at the same time.

pentatonic scale A five-tone scale using the pitches *do, re, mi, sol* and *la.*

perfect fifth An interval of two pitches that are five notes apart on a staff.

perfect fourth An interval of two pitches that are four notes apart on a staff.

phrase A musical idea with a beginning and an end.

phrasing A method of punctuating a musical idea, comparable to a line or sentence in poetry.

Phrygian scale *(FRIH-gee-an)* [Gk.] A modal scale that starts and ends on *mi.*

pianissimo *(pee-ah-NEE-see-moh)* [It.] A dynamic that indicates to sing or play very soft. (*pp*)

piano *(pee-AH-noh)* [It.] A dynamic that indicates to sing or play soft. (*p*)

Picardy third An interval of a major third used in the final, tonic chord of a piece written in a minor key.

pitch   Sound, the result of vibration; the highness or lowness of a tone, determined by the number of vibrations per second.

pitch matching   In a choral ensemble, the ability to sing the same notes as those around you.

più *(pyoo)*   [It.] More; for example, *più forte* means "more loudly."

più mosso *(pyoo MOHS-soh)*   [It.] A tempo marking that indicates "more motion," or faster.

poco *(POH-koh)*   [It.] Little; for example, *poco dim.* means "a little softer."

poco a poco *(POH-koh ah POH-koh)*   [It.] Little by little; for example, *poco a poco cresc.* means "little by little increase in volume."

polyphony *(pah-LIH-fun-nee)*   [Gk.] Literally, "many sounding." A type of music in which there are two or more different melodic lines being sung or played at the same time. Polyphony was refined during the Renaissance, and this period is sometimes called the "golden age of polyphony."

polyrhythms   A technique in which several different rhythms are performed at the same time.

portamento   A smooth and rapid glide from one note to another, executed continuously.

psalm   A sacred song or hymn. Specifically, one of the 150 Psalms in the Bible.

presto *(PREH-stoh)*   [It.] Very fast.

program music   A descriptive style of music composed to relate or illustrate a specific incident, situation or drama; the form of the piece is often dictated or influenced by the nonmusical program. This style commonly occurs in music composed during the Romantic period.

Q

quarter note   A note that represents one beat of sound when the quarter note receives the beat.

quarter note triplet   Three equal divisions of a half note.

quarter rest   A rest that represents one beat of silence when the quarter note receives the beat.

quartet   A group of four singers or instrumentalists.

R

rallentando *(rall.)* *(rahl-en-TAHN-doh)*   [It.] Meaning to "perform more and more slowly." *See also* ritard.

refrain   A repeated section at the end of each phrase or verse in a song. Also known as a *chorus*.

register, vocal   A term used for different parts of the singer's range, such as head register, or head voice (high notes); and chest register, or chest voice (low notes).

relative minor scale   A minor scale that shares the same key signature as its corresponding major scale. Both scales share the same half steps: between *mi* and *fa*, and *ti* and *do*.

Renaissance period   The historical period in Western civilization from 1430 to 1600.

repeat sign   A symbol that indicates that a section of music should be repeated.

repetition   The restatement of a musical idea; repeated pitches; repeated "A" section in ABA form.

requiem *(REK-wee-ehm)*   [Lt.] Literally, "rest." A mass written and performed to honor the dead and comfort the living.

resolution   The progression of chords or notes from the dissonant to the consonant, or point of rest.

resonance   Reinforcement and intensification of sound by vibration.

rest A symbol used in music notation to indicate silence.

rhythm The combination of long and short notes and rests in music. These may move with the beat, faster than the beat or slower than the beat.

ritard *(rit.) (ree-TAHRD)* [It.] A tempo marking that indicates to gradually get slower.

Romantic period The historical period in Western civilization from 1820 to 1900.

Romantic style In music history, the Romantic period dates from 1820 to 1900, following the Classical period. The word *romantic* (in music, as in art and literature) has to do with romance, imagination, strangeness and fantasy. Music composed in the *Romantic style*, when compared with the balance and restraint of the *Classical style*, is freer and more subjective, with increasing use of chromaticism.

rondo form A form in which a repeated section is separated by several contrasting sections.

rote The act of learning a song by hearing it over and over again.

round *See* canon.

rubato *(roo-BAH-toh)* [It.] The freedom to slow down and/or speed up the tempo without changing the overall pulse of a piece of music.

S

sacred music Music associated with religious services or themes.

scale A group of pitches that are sung or played in succession and are based on a particular home tone, or keynote.

scat singing An improvisational style of singing that uses nonsense syllables instead of words. It was made popular by jazz trumpeter Louis Armstrong.

Schubertiad Gatherings held in the homes of Viennese middle-class families; they featured amateur performances of songs and instrumental works by Franz Schubert (1797–1828).

score A notation showing all parts of a musical ensemble, with the parts stacked vertically and rhythmically aligned.

sea chantey A song sung by sailors, usually in rhythm with their work.

second The interval between two consecutive degrees of the diatonic scale.

secular music Music not associated with religious services or themes.

sempre *(SEHM-preh)* [It.] Always, continually.

sempre accelerando *(sempre accel.)* *(SEHM-preh ahk-chel)* [It.] A term that indicates to gradually increase the tempo of a piece or section of music.

sequence A successive musical pattern that begins on a higher or lower pitch each time it is repeated.

serenata [It.] A large-scale musical work written in honor of a special occasion. Generally performed in the evening or outside, it is often based on a mythological theme.

seventh The interval between the first and seventh degrees of the diatonic scale.

sforzando *(sfohr-TSAHN-doh)* [It.] A sudden strong accent on a note or chord. *(sfz)*

sharp A symbol that raises the pitch of a given note one half step. (♯)

sight-sing Reading and singing music at first sight.

simile *(sim.) (SIM-ee-leh)* [It.] To continue the same way.

simple meter Any meter in which the quarter note receives the beat, and the division of the beat is based on two eighth notes. 2/4, 3/4 and 4/4 are examples of simple meter.

singing posture The way one sits or stands while singing.

Singspiel *(ZEENG-shpeel)* [Ger.] A light German opera with spoken dialogue; e.g., Mozart's *The Magic Flute*.

sixteenth note A note that represents one quarter beat of sound when the quarter note receives the beat. Four sixteenth notes equal one beat of sound when the quarter note receives the beat.

sixteenth rest A rest that represents one quarter beat of silence when the quarter note receives the beat. Four sixteenth rests equal one beat of silence when the quarter note receives the beat.

skipwise motion The movement from a given note to another note that is two or more notes above or below it on the staff.

slur A curved line placed over or under a group of notes to indicate that they are to be performed without a break.

solfège syllables Pitch names using *do, re, mi, fa, sol, la, ti, do,* etc.

solo One person singing or playing an instrument alone.

sonata-allegro form A large ABA form consisting of three sections: exposition, development and recapitulation. This form was made popular during the Classical period.

soprano The highest-sounding female voice.

sostenuto *(SAHS-tuh-noot-oh)* [It.] The sustaining of a tone or the slackening of tempo.

sotto voce In a quiet, subdued manner; "under" the voice.

spirito *(SPEE-ree-toh)* [It.] Spirited; for example, *con spirito* ("with spirit").

spiritual Songs that were first sung by African American slaves, usually based on biblical themes or stories.

staccato *(stah-KAH-toh)* [It.] A short and detached style of singing or playing.

staff A series of five horizontal lines and four spaces on which notes are written. A staff is like a ladder. Notes placed higher on the staff sound higher than notes placed lower on the staff.

stage presence A performer's overall appearance on stage, including enthusiasm, facial expression and posture.

staggered breathing In ensemble singing, the practice of planning breaths so that no two singers take a breath at the same time, thus creating the overall effect of continuous singing.

staggered entrances A technique in which different parts and voices enter at different times.

stanza A section in a song in which the words change on each repeat. Also known as a *verse*.

stepwise motion The movement from a given note to another note that is directly above or below it on the staff.

straight tone A singing technique that uses minimal vocal vibrato.

strophe A verse or stanza in a song.

strophic A form in which the melody repeats while the words change from verse to verse.

style The particular character of a musical work, often indicated by words at the beginning of a composition, telling the performer the general manner in which the piece is to be performed.

subdominant chord A chord built on the fourth note of a scale. In a major scale, this chord uses the notes *fa, la* and *do,* and it may be called the **IV** ("four") chord, since it is based on the fourth note of the major scale, or *fa*. In a minor scale, this chord uses the notes *re, fa* and *la,* and it may be called the **iv** ("four") chord, since it is based on the fourth note of the minor scale, or *re*.

subito (sub.) *(SOO-bee-toh)* [It.] Suddenly.

subject The main musical idea in a fugue.

suspension The holding over of one or more musical tones in a chord into the following chord, producing a momentary discord.

swell A somewhat breathy, sudden crescendo. It is often used in gospel music.

swing rhythms Rhythms in which the second eighth note of each beat is played or sung like the last third of triplet, creating an uneven, "swing" feel. A style often found in jazz and blues. Swing rhythms are usually indicated at the beginning of a song or section.

syllabic *See* syllabic singing.

syllabic singing A style of text setting in which one syllable is sung on each note.

syllabic stress The stressing of one syllable over another.

symphonic poem A single-movement work for orchestra, inspired by a painting, play or other literary or visual work. Franz Liszt was a prominent composer of symphonic poems. Also known as a *tone poem.*

symphony A large-scale work for orchestra.

syncopation The placement of accents on a weak beat or a weak portion of the beat, or on a note or notes that normally do not receive extra emphasis.

synthesizer A musical instrument that produces sounds electronically, rather than by the physical vibrations of an acoustic instrument.

T

tag The ending of a barbershop song, usually the last four to eight bars, often considered the best chords in the song.

tamburo *(tahm-BOO-roh)* [It.] A two-headed drum played horizontally on the player's lap.

tempo Terms in music that indicate how fast or slow to sing or play.

tempo I or tempo primo *See* a tempo.

tenor The highest-sounding male voice.

tenuto *(teh-NOO-toh)* [It.] A symbol placed above or below a given note indicating that the note should receive stress and/or that its value should be slightly extended.

terraced dynamics Sudden and abrupt dynamic changes between loud and soft.

tessitura *(tehs-see-TOO-rah)* [It.] The average highness or lowness in pitch of a vocal piece.

text Words, usually set in a poetic style, that express a central thought, idea or narrative.

texture The thickness of the different layers of horizontal and vertical sounds.

theme A musical idea, usually a melody.

theme and variation form A musical form in which variations of the basic theme make up the composition.

third An interval of two pitches that are three notes apart on a staff.

tie A curved line used to connect two or more notes of the same pitch together in order to make one longer note.

tied notes Two or more notes of the same pitch connected together with a tie in order to make one longer note.

timbre The tone quality of a person's voice or musical instrument.

time signature The set of numbers at the beginning of a piece of music. The top number indicates the number of beats per measure. The bottom number indicates the kind of note that receives the beat. Time signature is sometimes called *meter signature.*

to coda Skip to (✛) or CODA.

tonality The relationship of a piece of music to its *keynote* (tonic).

tone color That which distinguishes the voice or tone of one singer or instrument from another; for example, a soprano from an alto, or a flute from a clarinet. *See also* timbre.

tonic chord A chord built on the home tone, or keynote, of a scale. In a major scale, this chord uses the notes *do, mi* and *sol,* and it may be called the **I** ("one") chord, since it is based on the first note of the major scale, or *do.* In a minor scale, this chord uses the notes *la, do* and *mi,* and it may be called the **i** ("one") chord, since it is based on the first note of the minor scale, or *la.*

treble clef A clef that generally indicates notes that sound higher than middle C.

trio A group of three singers or instrumentalists with usually one on a part.

triple A grouping of notes in equal sets of three.

triplet A group of notes in which three notes of equal duration are sung in the time normally given to two notes of equal duration.

troppo *(TROHP-oh)* [It.] Too much; for example, *allegro non troppo* ("not too fast").

tutti *(TOO-tee)* [It.] Meaning "all" or "together."

twelve-tone music A type of music that uses all twelve tones of the scale equally. Developed in the early twentieth century, Arnold Schoenberg is considered to be the pioneer of this style of music.

two-part music A type of music in which two different parts are sung or played.

U

unison All parts singing or playing the same notes at the same time.

upbeat One or more notes of a melody that occur before the first barline or which fall on a weak beat that leans toward the strong beat.

V

vaccin An instrument consisting of one or two sections of bamboo, blown with the lips like one would play the mouthpiece of a brass instrument. Also called a *bambou.*

vibrato *(vee-BRAH-toh)* [It.] A fluctuation of pitch on a single note, especially by singers and string players.

variation A modification of a musical idea, usually after its initial appearance in a piece.

villancico *(bee-ahn-SEE-koh)* [Sp.] A Spanish musical and poetic form consisting of several verses linked by a refrain. In modern-day Spain and Latin America, the term *villancico* usually means simply "Christmas carol."

vivace *(vee-VAH-chay)* [It.] Very fast; lively.

vocal jazz A popular style of music characterized by strong prominent meter, improvisation and dotted or syncopated patterns. Sometimes sung *a cappella.*

W

whole note A note that represents four beats of sound when the quarter note receives the beat.

whole rest A rest that represents four beats of silence when the quarter note receives the beat.

whole step The combination of two successive half steps.

word painting A technique in which the music reflects the meaning of the words.

word stress The act of singing important parts of the text in a more accented style than the other parts.

Classified Index

A Cappella

Benedicamus Domino 18

Dörven Dalai 164

Flower Of Beauty 12

Il est bel et bon 72

I'm Gonna Sing 'Til The Spirit
Moves In My Heart 172

Lux Aurumque 50

Noèl Ayisyen 58

Pingos D'água 208

A Rose Touched By The Sun's
Warm Rays 216

Set Me As A Seal 220

Somewhere 236

Sorida 246

Broadway

Somewhere 236

Composers

Pierre Passereau (c. 1509–1547)
Il est bel et bon 72

Antonio Vivaldi (1678–1741)
Domine Fili Unigenite 82

Wolfgang Amadeus Mozart (1756–1791)
Sancta Maria, mater Dei, K. 273 94

Robert Schumann (1810–1856)
Zigeunerleben 106

Randall Thompson (1899–1984)
The Last Words Of David 198

Jean Berger (1909–2002)
A Rose Touched By The Sun's
Warm Rays 216

Leonard Bernstein (1908–1990)
Somewhere 236

Henrique de Curitiba (b. 1934)
Pingos D'água 208

Yongrub (b. 1934)
Dörven Dalai 164

John Rutter (b. 1945)
What Sweeter Music 34

Javier Busto (b. 1949)
Ave Maria 158

David Dickau (b. 1953)
If Music Be The Food Of Love 186

Moses Hogan (1957–2003)
I'm Gonna Sing 'Til The Spirit
Moves In My Heart 172

Eric Whitacre (b. 1970)
Lux Aurumque 50

Folk

Jewish
S'vivon 44

Mongolian
Dörven Dalai 164

Foreign Language

French
Il est bel et bon 72

German
Zigeunerleben 106

Haitian
Noèl Ayisyen 58

Hebrew
S'vivon 44

Latin
Ave Maria 158

Benedicamus Domino 18

Domine Fili Unigenite 82

Lux Aurumque 50

Sancta Maria, mater Dei, K. 273 94

Mongolian
Dörven Dalai 164

Portuguese
Pingos D'água 208

Shona (Zimbabwe)
Sorida 246

Gospel/Spirituals

I'm Gonna Sing 'Til The Spirit
Moves In My Heart 172

No Rocks A-Cryin' 26

Instruments

Organ

Ave Maria 158

Jubilate Deo 2

Sancta Maria, mater Dei, K. 273 94

Percussion

Sorida 246

Music & History

Renaissance

Is est bel et bon 72

Baroque

Domine Fili Unigenite 82

Classical

Sancta Maria, mater Dei, K. 273 94

Romantic

Zigeunerleben 106

Contemporary

Ave Maria 158

Dörven Dalai 164

If Music Be The Food Of Love 186

I'm Gonna Sing 'Til The Spirit
Moves In My Heart 172

Jubilate Deo 2

The Last Words Of David 198

Lux Aurumque 50

Pingos D'água 208

A Rose Touched By The Sun's
Warm Rays 216

Somewhere 236

What Sweeter Music 34

Poetry

America, The Beautiful 146

Flower Of Beauty 12

If Music Be The Food Of Love 186

A Rose Touched By The Sun's
Warm Rays 216

Set Me As A Seal 220

What Sweeter Music 34

Seasonal, Patriotic

America, The Beautiful 146

Ave Maria 158

Lux Aurumque 50

Noèl Ayisyen 58

S'vivon 44

What Sweeter Music 34

Vocal Jazz

Skylark 226

Listening Lessons

L'incoronzione di Poppea, Act III,
Scene 8
Claudio Monteverdi 127

"Kyrie Eleison" from *Mass in B Minor*
Johann Sebastian Bach 131

"Laudate Dominum" from
Vesperae solemnes de confessore, K. 339
Wolfgang Amadeus Mozart 135

Symphony #9 in D Minor,
Fourth Movement
Ludwig van Beethoven 139

"Sanctus" from *Requiem*
Maurice Duruflé 143

Index of Songs and Spotlights

America, The Beautiful 146

Ave Maria 158

Benedicamus Domino 18

Domine Fili Unigenite 82

Dörven Dalai 164

Flower Of Beauty 12

I'm Gonna Sing 'Til The Spirit Moves In My Heart 172

If Music Be The Food Of Love 186

Il est bel et bon 72

Jubilate Deo 2

The Last Words Of David 198

Lux Aurumque 50

No Rock's A-Cryin' 26

Noèl Ayisyen 58

Pingos D'água 208

A Rose Touched By The Sun's Warm Rays 216

S'vivon 44

Sancta Maria, mater Dei, K. 273 94

Set Me As A Seal 220

Skylark 226

Somewhere 236

Sorida 246

What Sweeter Music 34

Zigeunerleben 106

Spotlights

Arranging 105

Careers In Music 185

Concert Etiquette 122

Gospel Music 43

Improvisation 215

Musical Theater 144

Physiology Of Singing 57

Physilogy Of The Voice 25

Vocal Health 245

Vocal Jazz 235

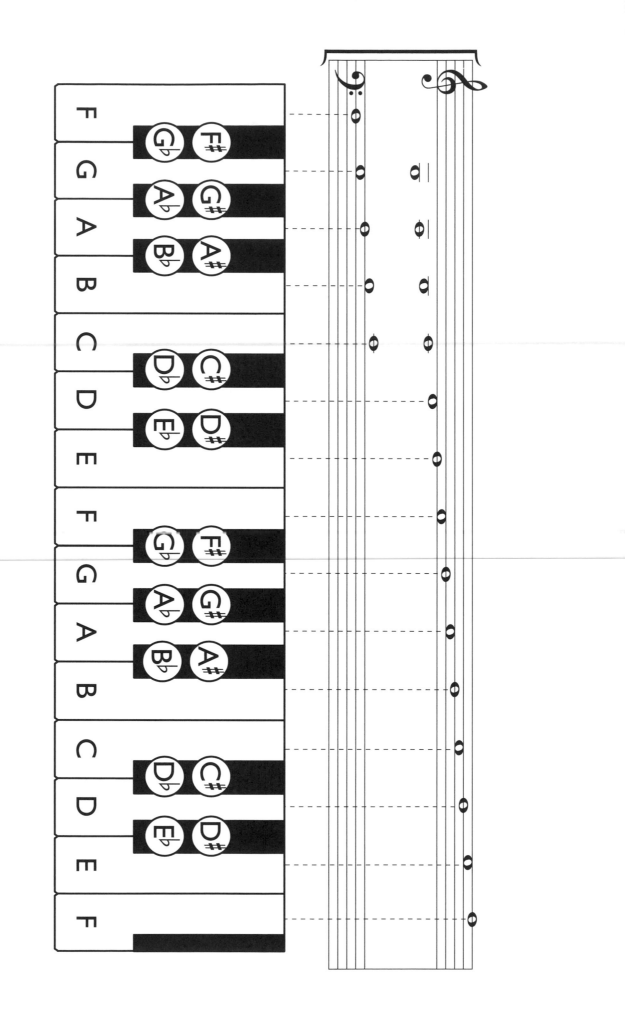